WORLD ATLAS

SPINNING GLOBE

Sarah Levete

Silver Dolphin Books
An imprint of the Advantage Publishers Group
5880 Oberlin Drive, San Diego, CA 92121-4794
SilverDolphin www.silverdolphinbooks.com

ISBN-13: 978-1-59223-643-5
ISBN-10: 1-59223-643-X

Made in Singapore
1 2 3 4 5 11 10 09 08 07

All maps and globes created by Digital Wisdom Publishing Ltd, except:
pages 9 and 13 Hardlines Ltd.

Picture credits
All images courtesy of Dreamstime except: Front/back cover tl corner Digital Vision; front/back cover
center NASA; front/back/inside box Digital Vision; front/back/inside box center NASA; back/front box
spine tl NASA; 6tr Dreamstime.com/Paul Brian; 10tr Alamy/Classic Image; 10br NASA; 14t
Dreamstime.com/Nicola Gavin;14br Dreamstime.com; 17tl ITN Stills Archive; 17tc courtesy of John
Deere; 17tr Dreamstime.com/Peter Weber; 18b Dreamstime.com/Anthony Hathaway; 18bl
Dreamstime.com/Graça Victoria; 20tl Stock.xchng; 20b Tall Tree Ltd.; 20br Jean Richards; 22b Tall Tree
Ltd.; 22bl Dreamstime.com/Christina Craft; 22br Tall Tree Ltd.; 25tl istockphoto.com; 25tr
Dreamstime.com/Carolyne Pehora; 25cl istockphoto.com; 25b Dreamstime.com/Pavalanche Stelian;
26br Getty/Tim Graham; 29tl Dreamstime.com/Jorge Felix Costa; 29cl Getty Images/Businesswire; 29b
Stock.xchng; 30b Dreamstime.com/Elpis Ioannidis; 32c Dreamstime.co/Alessandro Bolis; 32bl
Dreamstime.com/Dario Diament; 34tr Getty Images/Per-Anders Pettersson; 34b Digital Vision; 34br
Getty Images/Per-Anders Pettersson; 36tr Getty Images/Chris Hondros; 36b Digital Vision; 36bl
istockphoto.com; 38tr Dreamstime.com/Wang Sanjun; 38b Dreamstime.com/Youssouf Cader; 38br
Dreamstime.com/Bartlomiej Kwieciszewski; 41tl Dreamstime.com/Andreas Weiss; 41tr
Dreamstime.com/Graça Victoria; 41b Dreamstime.com/Jose Fuente; 42tr Dreamstime.com/Micha
Fleuren; 42br Dreamstime.com/Adrian Hillman; 45tl Getty Images/Rabih Moghrabi/AFP; 45tr Getty
Images/Steve Finn; 45cr Dreamstime.com/Marcus Brown; 45b Dreamstime.com/Holger Feroudj; 46tr
Getty Images/Nicole Duplaix/National Geographic; 46c Dreamstime.com/Georg Hafner; 46bl Digital
Vision; 46br Dreamstime.com/Joanne Harris; 48tr Dreamstime.com/Jan Will; 48c Dreamstime.com/Jan
Will; 48bl Dreamstime.com/Anthony Hathaway; 48br Getty Images

CONTENTS

HOW TO USE THIS ATLAS

GO ON A JOURNEY OF DISCOVERY around the world with this interactive 3-D guide to our planet. The pages of the atlas explain the geography, history, and culture of each region, while the corresponding fold-out maps show all the key geographical and political features. By spinning the globe, you can locate the region you've been studying.

Spin the globe and find . . .

This interactive section will test your knowledge of our planet.

- Use the globe and the maps to answer the questions.
- The answers can be found at the bottom of page 53.

CLICK IT
Click the two halves of the globe together, making sure that they match.

FIT IT
Slide the spindle through the ring binder and into the globe to fix it in place.

SPIN IT
Spin the globe to find the geographical region featured in each section.

STAND IT
Use the stand to position the globe at the same angle as the earth's axis.

Fact-filled introduction to each region gives key geographical and historical information

Interactive quizzes to test your knowledge

NORTHERN

SOUTHERN

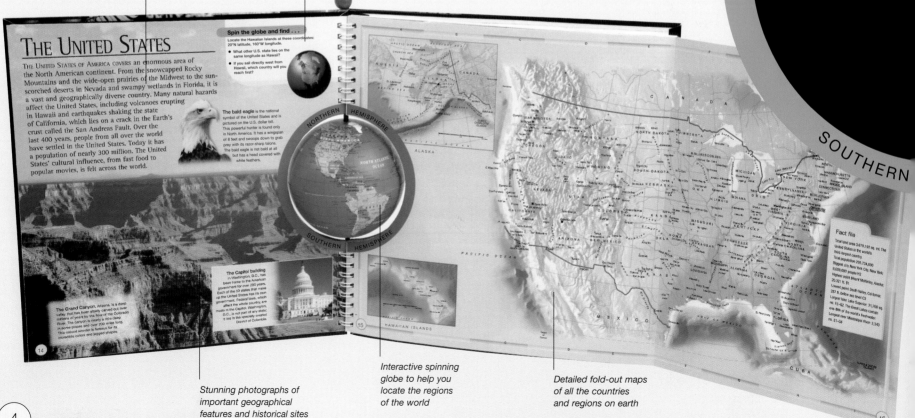

Stunning photographs of important geographical features and historical sites

Interactive spinning globe to help you locate the regions of the world

Detailed fold-out maps of all the countries and regions on earth

HOW TO USE THE GLOBE

The type of map shown on the globe is called a political map. It gives the names of the different continents and shows national boundaries and important cities as well as physical features such as oceans, mountains, and rivers.

KEY TO GLOBE

Continent	N O R T H A M E R I C A
Country	UNITED STATES
Capital city	✪ Washington
Major city/town	Atlanta

The names on the globe are displayed in different ways, depending on whether the name is that of a city, country, or continent. The key above shows how each is displayed.

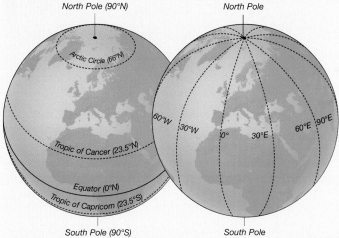

North Pole (90°N) — North Pole
Arctic Circle (66°N)
Tropic of Cancer (23.5°N)
60°W 30°W 0° 30°E 60°E 90°E
Equator (0°N)
Tropic of Capricorn (23.5°S)
South Pole (90°S) — South Pole

On the globe and the maps you will see vertical lines that meet at the North and South poles, and horizontal lines running parallel to the equator. These imaginary lines divide up the surface of the earth and are there to help us locate places and measure distances. The vertical lines indicate longitude; the horizontal ones indicate latitude. The position of each longitude line is measured by its distance from the prime meridian, which runs through Greenwich, England, and lies at 0°. The latitude lines are measured by their distance from the equator, which lies at 0°.

KEY TO FOLD-OUT MAPS

Maps are divided by imaginary grids to help you find the places you are looking for. In this atlas, the squares in the grid are labeled with letters along the top and bottom, and numbers running down the sides. To find a particular place, look it up in the map reference section. This will give you a page number and a grid reference—one letter and one number. Turn to the page where the place appears, then look for the square where the letter and number intersect.

CITIES AND TOWNS

⬤★ **National capital**
City where the country's government meets

★ **Local capital**
Major city or town where the government of a state, territory, or province meets

⬤ **City/major town**
Largest towns in a region

BOUNDARIES

▬▬ **International boundary**
Boundary between two countries

▬▬▬ **Internal boundary**
Boundary between states, territories, or provinces

PHYSICAL FEATURES

 Lakes
Large body of freshwater

Rivers
Path of a major river

▲ **Mountain peak**
Important mountain

 Mountainous areas
A mountain chain

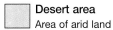 **Desert area**
Area of arid land

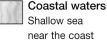 **Coastal waters**
Shallow sea near the coast

 Deep waters
Ocean far from the coast

Ice cap
Frozen area at a pole

SCALE

0   500   1000   1500 Miles

To determine the real distance between two places, measure the distance on the map with a ruler, then hold your ruler against the scale bar and calculate the number of miles.

SHOWING THE WORLD

THE WORLD IS DIVIDED into huge landmasses called continents. These have been shaped over millions of years, and they continue to move very slowly each year on large, interlocking pieces of the Earth's crust, called plates. The seven continents are Africa, Antarctica, Asia, Australia, Europe, North America, and South America. Continents can then be divided into countries. Countries are further divided into smaller areas, known as regions, states, territories, or counties.

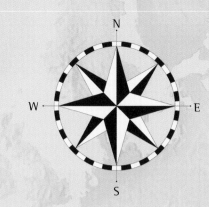

A state, province, or county covers part of a country. The state of Texas is part of the United States.

A country covers part of a continent. The United States covers the central part of North America.

A continent is a large, continuous piece of land, in this case, North America.

NORTHERN

SOUTHERN

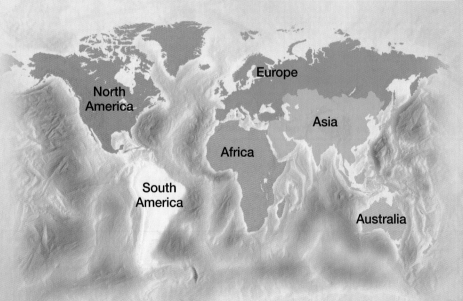

The continents vary greatly in size. For example, Asia is nearly five times the size of Australia. Their definitions can also vary. For instance, Europe and Asia can be merged into another continent, called Eurasia, while Australia can be included with New Zealand and the Pacific islands to form a continent called Australasia or Oceania.

A map of the U.S.
Scale 1:16,000,000

SCALE

A map shows information about a particular area at a much smaller size. This reduced size is called the scale, and some maps will have a scale bar or a ratio to indicate how much land is being shown. A ratio has numbers to tell the reader how much the maps have been reduced. For example, a ratio of 1:10,000 means that 1 inch on the map represents 10,000 inches of land. The map above shows a section of the southeastern United States. It has been reduced to a ratio of 1:16,000,000, so 1 inch on the map represents approximately 250 miles of land.

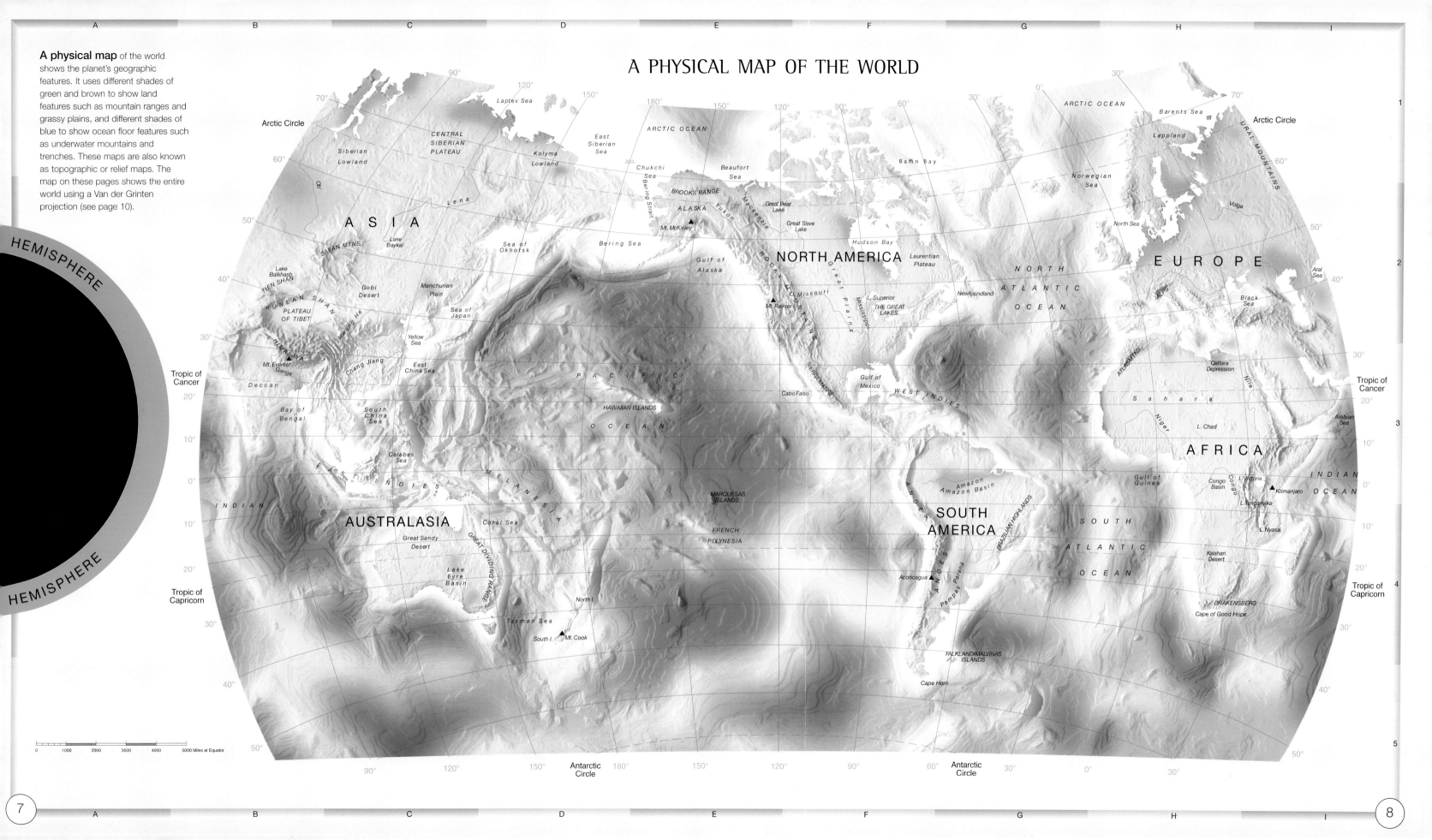

A PHYSICAL MAP OF THE WORLD

A physical map of the world shows the planet's geographic features. It uses different shades of green and brown to show land features such as mountain ranges and grassy plains, and different shades of blue to show ocean floor features such as underwater mountains and trenches. These maps are also known as topographic or relief maps. The map on these pages shows the entire world using a Van der Grinten projection (see page 10).

HEMISPHERE

HEMISPHERE

0   1000   2000   3000   4000   5000 Miles at Equator

ASIA

Arctic Circle

Siberian Lowland

CENTRAL SIBERIAN PLATEAU

Laptev Sea

Kolyma Lowland

East Siberian Sea

Chukchi Sea

ARCTIC OCEAN

Beaufort Sea

Baffin Bay

ARCTIC OCEAN

Barents Sea

Arctic Circle

Lappland

URAL MOUNTAINS

Norwegian Sea

Lena

Bering Strait

BROOKS RANGE

ALASKA

Yukon

Mackenzie

Great Bear Lake

Great Slave Lake

North Sea

Volga

Lake Baykal

Mt. McKinley

Sea of Okhotsk

Bering Sea

Gulf of Alaska

ROCKY MOUNTAINS

NORTH AMERICA

Hudson Bay

Laurentian Plateau

NORTH ATLANTIC OCEAN

EUROPE

Aral Sea

SAYAN MTNS.

TIEN SHAN

Lake Balkhash

Manchurian Plain

Mt. Rainier

Great Plains

Missouri

L. Superior
THE GREAT LAKES

Newfoundland

ALPS

Black Sea

KUNLAN SHAN

Gobi Desert

Sea of Japan

Mississippi

SIERRA MADRE

ATLAS MTNS.

Qattara Depression

PLATEAU OF TIBET

Hwang He

Yellow Sea

Gulf of Mexico

WEST INDIES

Nile

Tropic of Cancer

HIMALAYA

Mt. Everest

Ganga

Chang Jiang

East China Sea

PACIFIC

Cabo Falso

Sahara

Tropic of Cancer

Deccan

South China Sea

HAWAIIAN ISLANDS

OCEAN

Arabian Sea

Bay of Bengal

AFRICA

Celebes Sea

EAST INDIES

Gulf of Guinea

Congo Basin

Congo

L. Victoria

Kilimanjaro

INDIAN OCEAN

INDIAN

MELANESIA

Amazon

Amazon Basin

ANDES

L. Tanganyika

AUSTRALASIA

Coral Sea

MARQUESAS ISLANDS

SOUTH AMERICA

BRAZILIAN HIGHLANDS

L. Nyasa

SOUTH

Great Sandy Desert

GREAT DIVIDING RANGE

FRENCH POLYNESIA

SOUTH ATLANTIC OCEAN

Kalahari Desert

Lake Eyre Basin

Aconcagua

ANDES

Pampas

Paraná

DRAKENSBERG

Tropic of Capricorn

North I.

Tasman Sea

South I.

Mt. Cook

FALKLAND/MALVINAS ISLANDS

Cape of Good Hope

Tropic of Capricorn

Cape Horn

Antarctic Circle

Antarctic Circle

VEGETATION DISTRIBUTION MAP

Types of Vegetation

Temperate forest — Mediterranean scrub
Tropical grassland — Temperate grassland
Tropical forest — Desert

Swamp
Polar conditions

Mountain region
Tundra
Taiga

A vegetation distribution map shows the different vegetation zones, known as biomes, around the world. Different plants and animals have evolved their own unique methods for surviving in each biome. For example, cacti have thick leaves that can hold a lot of water and help the plant survive a dry period in a desert, while plants in rain forests have pointed leaves so that rainwater runs off and moss and mildew do not grow on them.

MAKING MAPS

THE FIRST MAPS were created around 2500 BC. These early maps were drawn by hand by people looking at the land, or else they drew them by hand from memory. Today's maps use the latest high-tech methods, such as satellites. Satellites can take very detailed photos and these can be turned into extremely accurate maps. These maps can then be used to show lots of different information, such as a region's geographical features or the borders of different countries. One of the biggest problems for mapmakers is how to show the entire planet accurately on a map. The world is three-dimensional and shaped like a ball, but maps are two-dimensional and flat.

PROJECTIONS

Because maps are a two-dimensional version of the three-dimensional world, they will distort the look and shape of the land being shown. Mapmakers have used a number of different views, or projections, in order to make the maps as accurate as possible. Some projections show only a part of the whole world, while others spread the entire globe out flat.

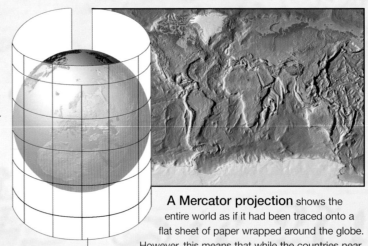

A Mercator projection shows the entire world as if it had been traced onto a flat sheet of paper wrapped around the globe. However, this means that while the countries near the equator would be shown accurately, those near the poles would be distorted. For example, Greenland appears to be larger than South America when it actually has a smaller land area.

A Mercator projection shows the world as if it has been unfolded onto a flat sheet.

An azimuthal projection is also called a plane projection. It shows a portion of the globe as if viewed from space, in this case Europe and northern Africa.

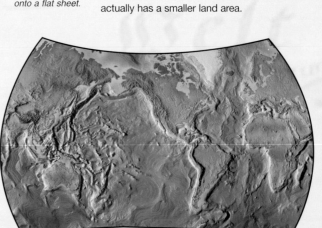

A Van der Grinten projection is a map of the whole world. By curving the edges of the map, the amount of area that is distorted in a Mercator projection is reduced.

Hand-drawn maps were as accurate as mapmakers could make at the time. The use of modern technology, such as satellites and computers, has replaced hand-drawn maps.

Satellites can take detailed photos such as this one of Mumbai, India. These can accurately show the countryside and can be used to make a map. Many satellites, such as NASA's Landsat satellites (pictured), are fitted with special cameras and sensors.

NORTHERN

SOUTHERN

Landsat satellite

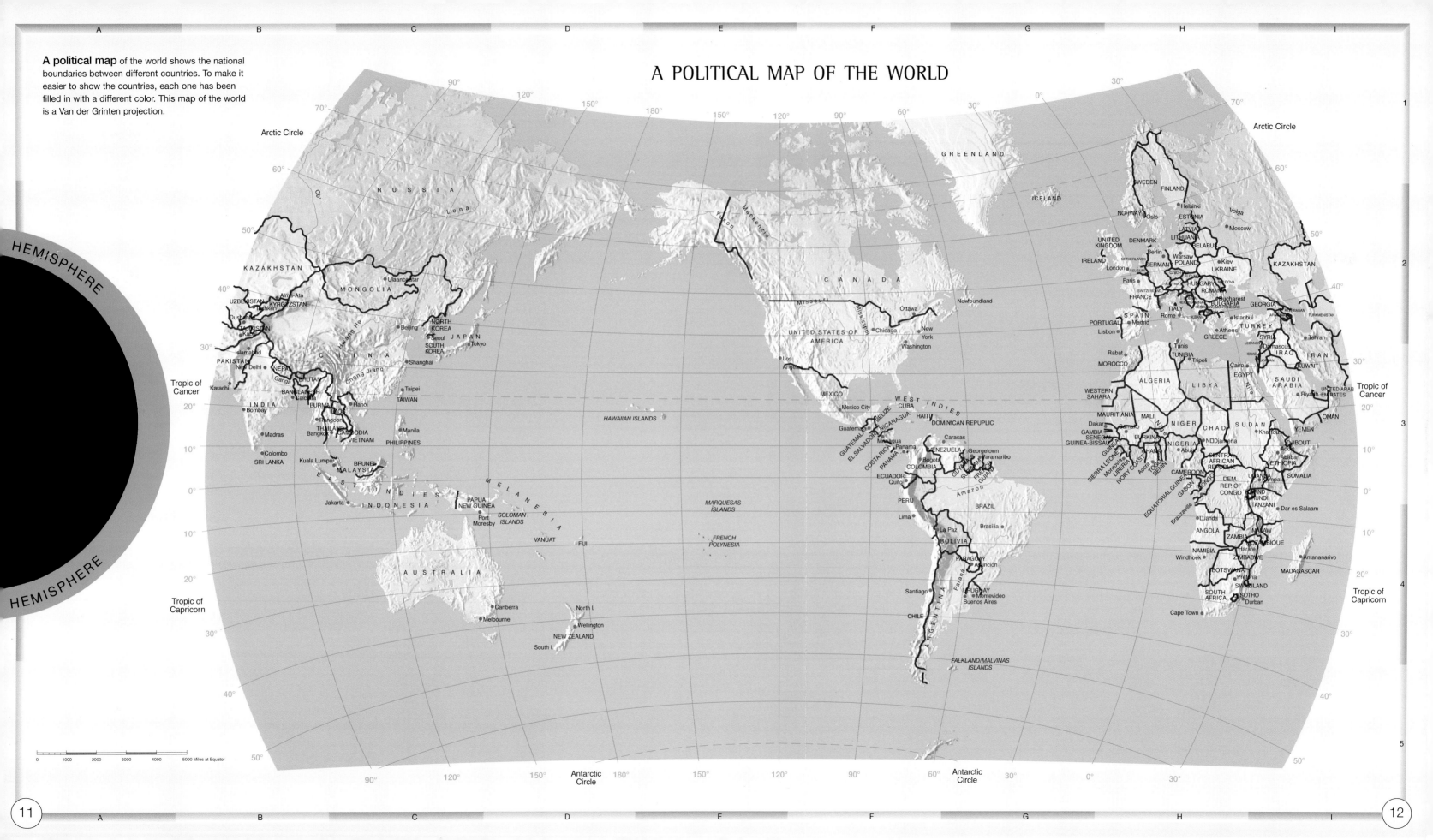

A POLITICAL MAP OF THE WORLD

A political map of the world shows the national boundaries between different countries. To make it easier to show the countries, each one has been filled in with a different color. This map of the world is a Van der Grinten projection.

HEMISPHERE

HEMISPHERE

0   1000   2000   3000   4000   5000 Miles at Equator

Arctic Circle

Arctic Circle

Tropic of Cancer

Tropic of Cancer

Tropic of Capricorn

Tropic of Capricorn

Antarctic Circle

Antarctic Circle

POPULATION DENSITY MAP

Population density per square mile

500
250
100
50
25
5
0

A population density map uses color coding to show the different densities of people living in various parts of the world today. Some areas of the world are very densely populated, with hundreds of people per square mile. These include parts of western Europe, India, and China. Other regions have very few people, such as the center of Australia, the Sahara in North Africa, and northern Canada.

THE UNITED STATES

THE UNITED STATES OF AMERICA COVERS an enormous area of the North American continent. From the snowcapped Rocky Mountains and the wide-open prairies of the Midwest to the sun-scorched deserts in Nevada and swampy wetlands in Florida, it is a vast and geographically diverse country. Many natural hazards affect the United States, including volcanoes erupting in Hawaii and earthquakes shaking the state of California, which lies on a crack in the Earth's crust called the San Andreas Fault. Over the last 400 years, people from all over the world have settled in the United States. Today it has a population of nearly 300 million. The United States' cultural influence, from fast food to popular movies, is felt across the world.

Spin the globe and find . . .

Locate the Hawaiian Islands at these coordinates: 20°N latitude, 160°W longitude.

- What other U.S. state lies on the same longitude as Hawaii?
- If you sail directly west from Hawaii, which country will you reach first?

The bald eagle is the national symbol of the United States and is pictured on the U.S. dollar bill. This powerful hunter is found only in North America. It has a wingspan of 8 feet and swoops down to grab prey with its razor-sharp talons. The bald eagle is not bald at all but has a head covered with white feathers.

NORTHERN

SOUTHERN

The Grand Canyon, Arizona, is a deep valley that has been slowly carved out over millions of years by the flow of the Colorado River. The canyon is nearly a mile deep in some places and over 200 miles long. This natural wonder is famous for its incredible colors and jagged shapes.

The Capitol building in Washington, D.C., has been home to the American government for over 200 years. Each of the 50 states that make up the United States has its own government. Federal laws, which affect the whole country, are made in the Capitol. Washington, D.C., is not part of any state; it lies in the specially created District of Columbia.

Fact file

Total land area 3,679,192 sq. mi. The United States is the world's third-largest country.

Total population 295,734,000

Biggest city New York City, New York: 8,000,000 people **H2**

Highest point Mount McKinley, Alaska: 20,321 ft. **B1**

Lowest point Death Valley, California: 287 ft. below sea level **C3**

Largest lake Lake Superior: 31,700 sq. mi. **F2–G2**. The Great Lakes contain one-fifth of the world's freshwater.

Longest river Mississippi River: 2,340 mi. **E1–G4**

The Statue of Liberty greets people as they sail into New York City's harbor. The copper-covered statue was a gift of friendship from the French to the Americans during the 1800s. It has become a symbol of freedom and democracy.

Baseball is played and watched by millions of Americans. Professional teams, such as the New York Yankees and Boston Red Sox, have thousands of loyal fans. At the end of each season, the top teams compete for the World Series trophy.

Martin Luther King Jr. was a key figure in the civil rights movement of the 1950s and 1960s. He campaigned for a nonviolent end to the racial discrimination suffered by black Americans. King was assassinated in 1968. Martin Luther King Day is now a national holiday to remember and celebrate his life.

The Great Plains that lie to the east of the Rocky Mountains are vast prairies of grassland. Many prairie plants have adapted to the long, dry summers, cold winters, and strong winds. Buffalo, elk, and deer used to graze on the open ground, but today this fertile area supports the United States' agricultural industry.

Tornadoes are columns of spinning air that produce violent winds with speeds of up to 300 mph. Tornadoes occur so regularly in the Midwest from Nebraska down to Texas that the area has earned the nickname "Tornado Alley."

Cape Canaveral in Florida is the main launch site for the United States' space missions. Since the 1960s, the United States has been at the forefront of space exploration, sending people to the International Space Station and launching space vehicles to explore the solar system.

CANADA AND GREENLAND

THE NORTHERN PARTS OF CANADA and Greenland lie inside the Arctic Circle, a region that surrounds the North Pole. This area is covered in thick ice for much of the year. Greenland is roughly twice the size of the state of Texas and it is the world's largest island. Here the climate is harsh and over 80 percent of Greenland is covered in ice that is 10 feet thick in places. Nearly 90 percent of Canadians live within 100 miles of the border with the United States in cities such as the capital, Ottawa. This leaves vast areas of empty wilderness to the north, much of which is covered in thick forest.

Spin the globe and find . . .

Locate Ottawa at these coordinates: 45°N latitude, 75°W longitude.

- Which ocean surrounds the island of Greenland?
- Apart from Canada and Greenland, what countries lie on the Arctic Circle?

The grizzly bear gets its name from the rough appearance of long white-tipped hairs on its back. Adult male bears can weigh 800 pounds—that is as much as five adult humans. Despite this, they can run at up to 40 miles per hour.

NORTHERN

SOUTHERN

The CN Tower in Toronto, Ontario, is the world's tallest freestanding structure. It was completed in February 1974 and is 1,843 feet tall. The skypod is situated 1,465 feet up and gives views of up to 75 miles away. The tower has been built to survive winds of 260 mph and an earthquake of 8.5 on the Richter scale.

Totem poles were originally made by the indigenous, or native, people of Canada. The poles are symbols and each pole tells a story about the people or their leader, or a legend relating to a particular animal. Today many indigenous people live and work in Greenland and Canada but struggle to preserve their language and traditional way of life.

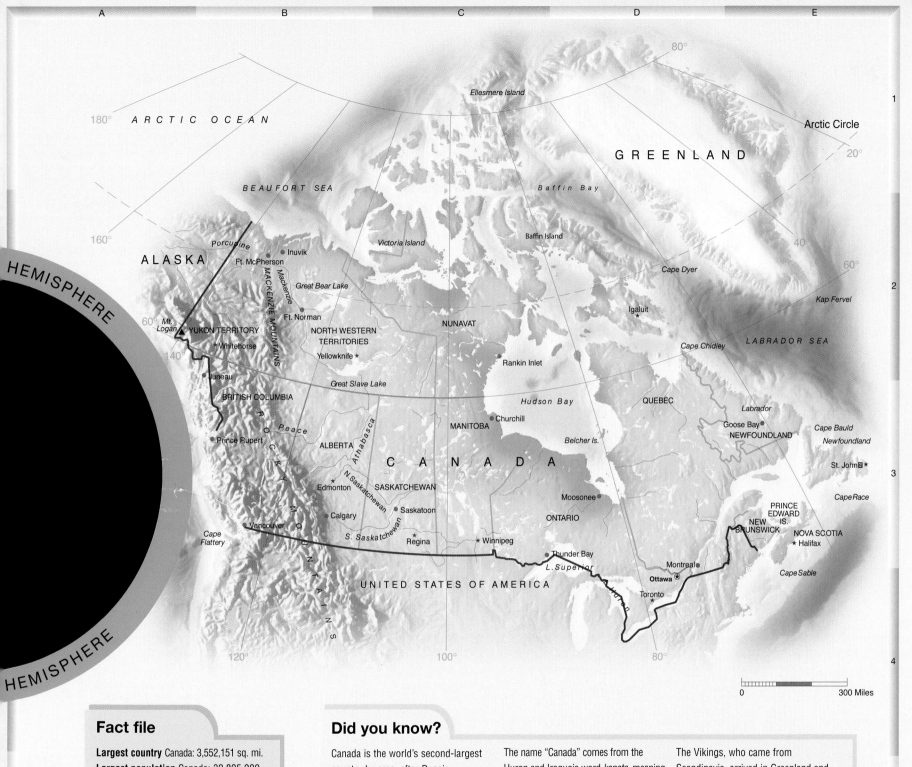

A B C D E

1

80°
ARCTIC OCEAN
Arctic Circle
180°
Ellesmere Island
20°
BEAUFORT SEA
Baffin Bay
GREENLAND
160°
Baffin Island
40°
Victoria Island
Cape Dyer
60°
Porcupine
Inuvik
ALASKA
Ft. McPherson
Kap Fervel

2
Great Bear Lake
NUNAVAT
Igaluit
LABRADOR SEA
Ft. Norman
60°
Mt.
Logan
YUKON TERRITORY
NORTH WESTERN
TERRITORIES
Cape Chidley
140°
Whitehorse
Yellowknife ★
Rankin Inlet
Juneau
Great Slave Lake
BRITISH COLUMBIA
Hudson Bay
QUEBEC
Labrador
Churchill
Goose Bay
Belcher Is.
NEWFOUNDLAND
Cape Bauld
Peace
MANITOBA
Newfoundland
Prince Rupert
ALBERTA
CANADA
Athabasca

3
St. Johns ★
Edmonton
N.Saskatchewan
SASKATCHEWAN
Moosonee
Cape Race
Calgary
Saskatoon
ONTARIO
PRINCE
EDWARD
IS.
Cape
Flattery
S. Saskatchewan
Regina
★ Winnipeg
Vancouver
NEW
BRUNSWICK
NOVA SCOTIA
Thunder Bay
Montreal
★ Halifax
L. Superior
Ottawa ✪
Cape Sable
UNITED STATES OF AMERICA
Toronto

4
120°
100°
80°

0   300 Miles

HEMISPHERE

HEMISPHERE

Fact file

Largest country Canada: 3,552,151 sq. mi.
Largest population Canada: 32,805,000
Biggest city Toronto, Canada: 2,500,000
people **D4**
Highest point Mount Logan, Canada:
19,863 ft. **A2**
Lowest point Atlantic Ocean: 0 ft.
Longest river Mackenzie River, Canada:
1,086 mi. **B2**

Did you know?

Canada is the world's second-largest country by area, after Russia.

Canada has the world's longest coastline. The coastline is 126,300 miles long and touches three oceans: the Pacific Ocean in the west, the Atlantic Ocean in the east, and the Arctic Ocean in the north.

The name "Canada" comes from the Huron and Iroquois word *kanata*, meaning "village." The Huron and Iroquois are indigenous peoples of North America.

Most people in Canada speak English as a first language. However, many people who live in the province of Quebec speak French as a first language.

The Vikings, who came from Scandinavia, arrived in Greenland and North America in the tenth century AD, nearly 500 years before Columbus.

Grise Ford, in the Canadian territory of Nunavut, is the northernmost city in the world. It lies 2,700 miles north of Ottawa and is home to just 130 people.

CENTRAL AMERICA

CENTRAL AMERICA IS THE THIN STRIP of land linking North and South America. The region has a rich history, and many civilizations flourished here before the arrival of European explorers in the 15th century. Today's inhabitants include descendants of indigenous peoples, European settlers, and African slaves who were brought to the region to work on plantations. The region's geography varies from the dry, dusty deserts of Mexico to the lush rain forests of Costa Rica. The Caribbean contains a chain of hundreds of islands featuring long, sandy beaches and deep blue seas. Many natural hazards affect Central America, such as powerful earthquakes, volcanoes, and raging hurricanes.

Colorful carnivals are a familiar sight in the Caribbean, celebrating a mixture of religious and social occasions, such as Shrove Tuesday, which is also known as Mardi Gras. People wear bright and colorful costumes and dance through the streets in long parades.

Spin the globe and find . . .

Locate the Panama Canal on these coordinates: 8°N latitude, 80°W longitude.

- What two bodies of water does the Panama Canal link?
- What U.S. state is closest to the island of Cuba?

NORTHERN

SOUTHERN

This pyramid is just one feature of the ruins of Chichén Itzá, an ancient city in the Yucatán Peninsula, Mexico. It was built by the Mayan civilization, which flourished in the region around AD 250–900. After 900, the Mayan civilization mysteriously declined and many of their cities were abandoned.

The Panama Canal runs across a narrow strip of land in Panama, carrying ships across Central America. It was opened in 1914 and can save nearly 8,000 nautical miles on a ship's journey between the Atlantic and Pacific oceans. Large ships that enter the canal are pulled through the system of locks by powerful railroad locomotives.

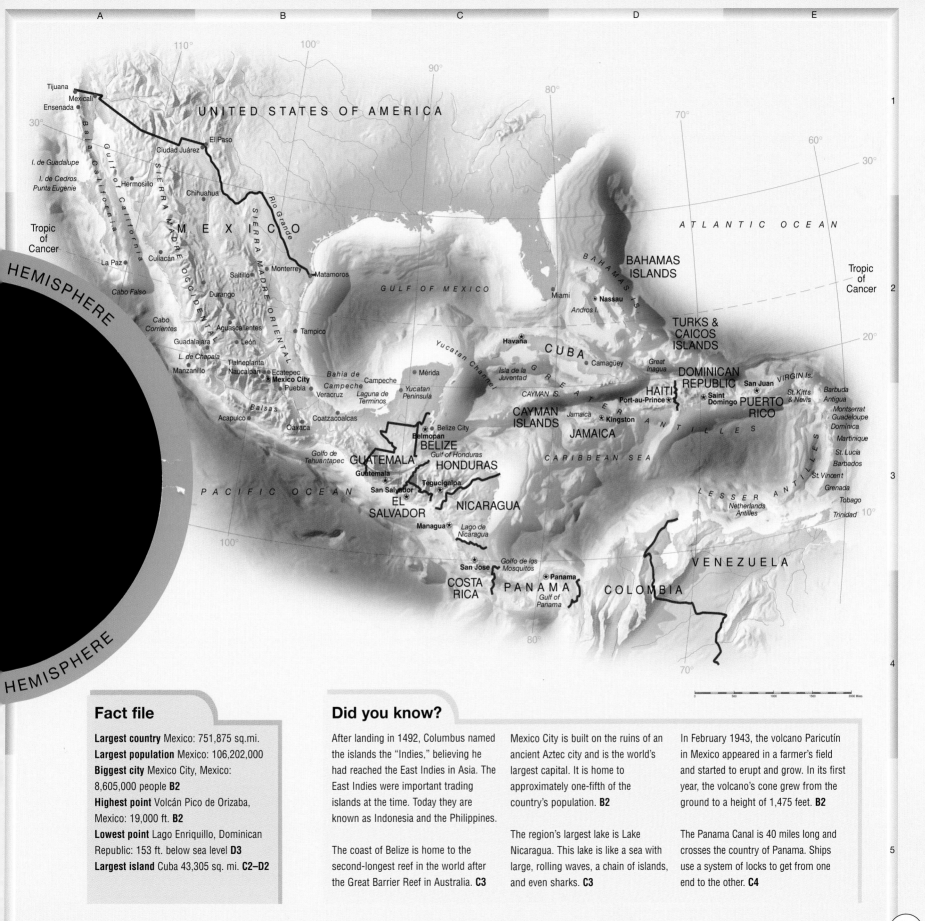

HEMISPHERE

HEMISPHERE

UNITED STATES OF AMERICA

ATLANTIC OCEAN

Tijuana
Mexicali
Ensenada
I. de Guadalupe
I. de Cedros
Punta Eugenie
El Paso
Ciudad Juárez
Chihuahua
Rio Grande
Hermosillo
La Paz
Cabo Falso
Culiacán
Saltillo
Monterrey
Matamoros
Durango
MEXICO
SIERRA MADRE ORIENTAL
SIERRA MADRE OCCIDENTAL
Gulf of California
Baja California
Tropic of Cancer
Cabo Corrientes
Aguascalientes
Tampico
GULF OF MEXICO
Guadalajara
León
L. de Chapala
Tlalneplanta
Manzanillo
Naucalpan
Ecatepec
Mexico City
Puebla
Bahia de Campeche
Campeche
Mérida
Veracruz
Laguna de Terminos
Yucatan Peninsula
Balsas
Acapulco
Oaxaca
Coatzacoalcas
Golfo de Tehuantepec
Belize City
Belmopan
BELIZE
GUATEMALA
Gulf of Honduras
Guatemala
HONDURAS
San Salvador
Tegucigalpa
EL SALVADOR
NICARAGUA
Managua
Lago de Nicaragua
San Jose
Golfo de los Mosquitos
COSTA RICA
PANAMA
Panama
Gulf of Panama
COLOMBIA
VENEZUELA

PACIFIC OCEAN

Yucatan Channel
Havana
CUBA
Miami
Nassau
BAHAMAS ISLANDS
Andros I.
Camagüey
Isla de la Juventad
CAYMAN IS.
Great Inagua
TURKS & CAICOS ISLANDS
DOMINICAN REPUBLIC
San Juan
VIRGIN Is.
HAITI
Port-au-Prince
Saint Domingo
PUERTO RICO
St. Kitts & Nevis
Barbuda
Antigua
Montserrat
Guadeloupe
Domínica
Martinique
St. Lucia
Barbados
St. Vincent
Grenada
Tobago
Trinidad
Netherlands Antilles
LESSER ANTILLES
GREATER ANTILLES
CAYMAN ISLANDS
Jamaica
Kingston
JAMAICA
CARIBBEAN SEA
Tropic of Cancer

Fact file

Largest country Mexico: 751,875 sq.mi.
Largest population Mexico: 106,202,000
Biggest city Mexico City, Mexico: 8,605,000 people **B2**
Highest point Volcán Pico de Orizaba, Mexico: 19,000 ft. **B2**
Lowest point Lago Enriquillo, Dominican Republic: 153 ft. below sea level **D3**
Largest island Cuba 43,305 sq. mi. **C2–D2**

Did you know?

After landing in 1492, Columbus named the islands the "Indies," believing he had reached the East Indies in Asia. The East Indies were important trading islands at the time. Today they are known as Indonesia and the Philippines.

The coast of Belize is home to the second-longest reef in the world after the Great Barrier Reef in Australia. **C3**

Mexico City is built on the ruins of an ancient Aztec city and is the world's largest capital. It is home to approximately one-fifth of the country's population. **B2**

The region's largest lake is Lake Nicaragua. This lake is like a sea with large, rolling waves, a chain of islands, and even sharks. **C3**

In February 1943, the volcano Paricutín in Mexico appeared in a farmer's field and started to erupt and grow. In its first year, the volcano's cone grew from the ground to a height of 1,475 feet. **B2**

The Panama Canal is 40 miles long and crosses the country of Panama. Ships use a system of locks to get from one end to the other. **C4**

SOUTH AMERICA

SOUTH AMERICA is a very long continent and stretches from above the equator down almost to Antarctica. One-third of South America is covered in dense rain forest, most of which lies around the Amazon River. This is one of the richest habitats in the world, home to 30 percent of all plant and animal life on Earth. However, the rain forests are threatened by human activities such as farming. There are also many large cities throughout South America, such as Rio de Janeiro and Buenos Aires. Many of these cities are popular tourist destinations with famous landmarks and beaches, such as Sugarloaf Mountain in Rio de Janeiro. About 600 miles off the coast of Ecuador are the Galápagos Islands. These islands are home to some amazing animals that are found nowhere else in the world, including marine iguanas and giant land tortoises.

Spin the globe and find . . .

Locate Rio de Janeiro at these coordinates: 22°S latitude, 43°W longitude.

- How many countries do the Andes mountains pass through?
- Into which ocean does the Amazon River empty?

The Amazon rain forest is divided horizontally into layers, each one the habitat for different plants and animals. The top layer is formed by high trees, called emergents, that reach up to 130 feet. Below this is an umbrella-like canopy of trees. Smaller trees and plants grow in the lower, shadier understory.

NORTHERN

SOUTHERN

This three-toed sloth lives in low-level tropical rain forests in South America. It hangs onto branches upside down and sleeps for most of the day. In fact, it spends about just 10 percent of its time moving. When it does move, it usually climbs very slowly through the branches to find leaves and shoots to eat. Green algae grows in the sloth's furry coat, helping to camouflage it from predators such as harpy eagles and jaguars.

Sugarloaf Mountain towers 1,300 feet over Rio de Janeiro, Brazil, and Copacabana beach. Rio's beaches attract thousands of tourists who are also drawn to Brazil's warm climate. The city is also the site of the world's biggest carnival. This four-day festival is held every year to celebrate Mardi Gras, which occurs just before the Christian period of Lent.

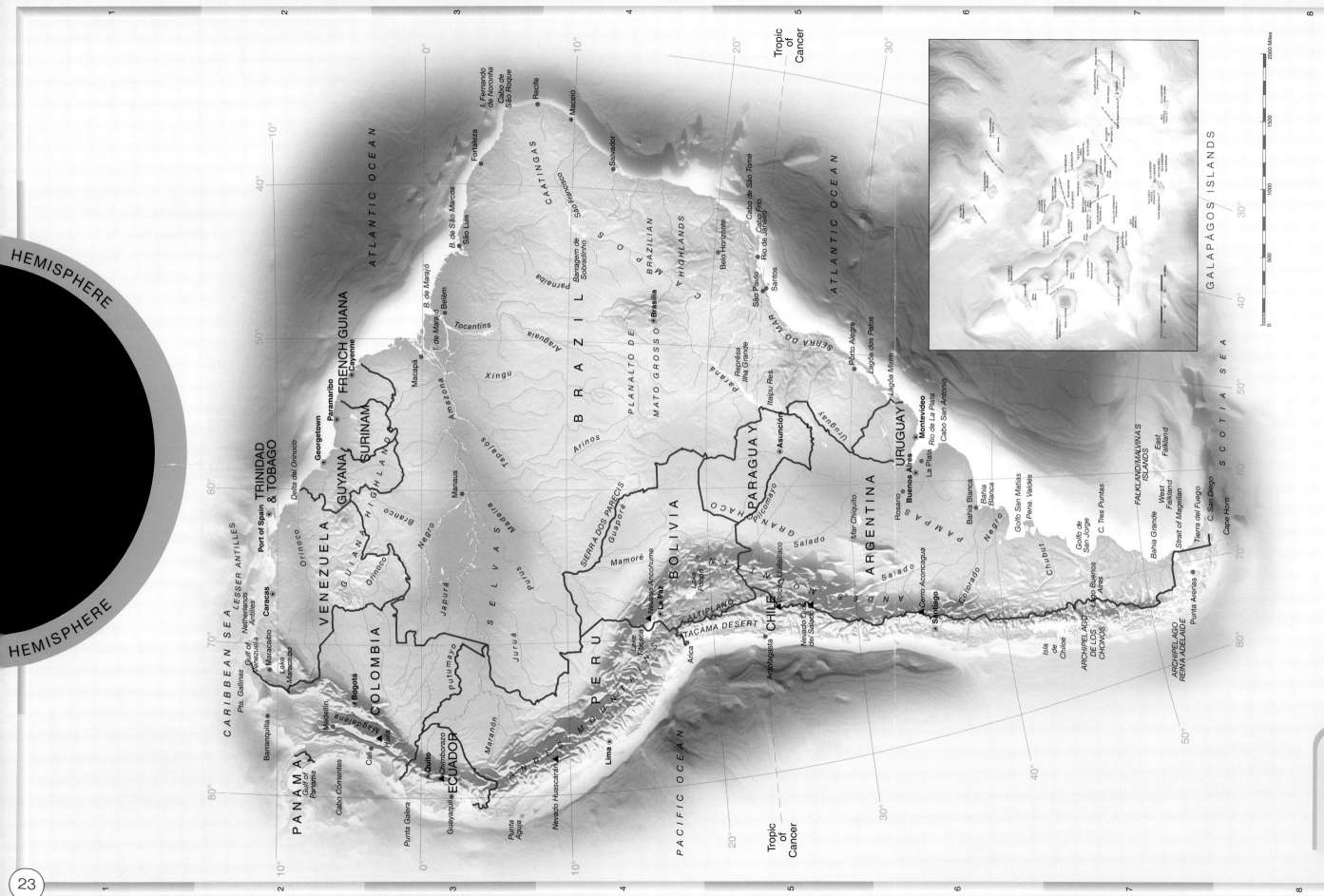

Fact file

Largest country Brazil: 3,280,000 sq. mi. Brazil is the world's fifth-largest country.
Largest population Brazil: 186,112,800
Biggest city São Paulo, Brazil: 10,333,200 people **D5**
Highest point Aconcagua, Andes mountains, Argentina: 22,831 ft. **B6**
Lowest point Península Valdés, Argentina: 151 ft. below sea level
Longest river Amazon River: 3,900 mi. **B4–D3**

Did you know?

The Amazon rain forest stretches from the Andes mountains to the Atlantic Ocean, covering 2.5 million square miles. In comparison, the area of the mainland U.S. is 3.7 million square miles.

The Bolivian city of La Paz is the highest capital in the world, sitting at 12,001 feet above sea level. **B4**

The trees in the rain forest recycle the gas carbon dioxide and turn it into oxygen, which is essential for every living organism. More than 20 percent of the world's oxygen is released by the Amazon rain forest.

The Brazilian capital city of Brasília was built in the shape of an airplane. **D4**

The Incas were a civilization that ruled a large part of South America. When the first European settlers arrived in the 1530s, the Incan empire was home to nearly 12 million people.

The Atacama Desert is the driest place on Earth. In some places, just 0.02 in of rain has fallen in nearly 40 years. **B4–B5**

23

24

Angel Falls, Venezuela, is the world's highest waterfall, with a drop of 3,212 feet. Indigenous people have known of the waterfall for thousands of years, calling it the "Devil's Mouth." The name Angel Falls was given after the waterfall was spotted by an American pilot named Jimmy Angel when he was flying nearby in 1937.

Llamas were used for transport and meat by the Incas, a civilization that lived in the Andes over 500 years ago. Today llamas are used as a source of milk, wool, and meat, and as pack animals, carrying loads up and down narrow mountain paths. Llama dung is also used as fuel for fires.

Gauchos are South American cattlemen, similar to North American cowboys. Many gauchos live on the flat plains, or pampas, of Argentina. Gauchos ride horses to round up beef cattle on the large ranches, or estancias, where they work.

Machu Picchu is an Incan site high up in the Andes in Peru. The Incas ruled an enormous empire that stretched throughout what is now Ecuador, Peru, Bolivia, and Chile. Machu Picchu remained hidden for hundreds of years until American Hiram Bingham came across the ruins in 1911. The site contains hundreds of terraces that are linked by thousands of steps.

WESTERN EUROPE

Spin the globe and find . . .

Locate London at these coordinates: 50°N latitude, 0°W longitude.

- What is Europe's westernmost capital city?
- Which mountain range separates the countries of France and Spain?

EUROPE IS ONE OF THE SMALLEST CONTINENTS, yet it is one of the most densely populated and wealthiest regions in the world. Its countries have a very long social and cultural history dating back thousands of years. Many of the cities in this region contain modern buildings and monuments alongside ancient castles, churches, and palaces. They also have museums with works of art that are hundreds of years old. Many of the countries in this region have joined together to form the European Union, or E.U., and some of these countries have even replaced their old money with a new common currency—the euro. The region stretches from the cold, bleak tundra of the Arctic Circle down to the warm lands just north of Africa. It has two large mountain ranges, the Alps and the Pyrenees, whose dramatic peaks are popular skiing destinations.

The Alps run through France, Switzerland, Austria, and Italy. These jagged peaks rise up to more than 15,000 feet and the summits are covered in snow all year round. Many mountain slopes have ski resorts that are popular with travelers.

NORTHERN

SOUTHERN

The London Eye is a huge Ferris wheel that was built to celebrate the new millennium. It lies on the south bank of the Thames River at the center of England's capital city. London was first founded over 2,000 years ago and today contains a mixture of old buildings, such as St. Paul's Cathedral, and new structures like the London Eye.

CITY CRUISES

Hot springs in Iceland are created by water bubbling up from warm volcanic rocks beneath the surface. Iceland is in the middle of the Atlantic Ocean, above an area with a lot of volcanic activity. This activity heats up any water that is trapped in the rocks. The hot water rises to form pools of warm water that people can swim in.

Did you know?

Iceland has about 800 hot springs, found in 250 areas, with an average water temperature of around 167°F. **A2**

The word "ski" comes from a Norwegian word meaning "a stick of wood." The first skis were made over 5,000 years ago.

The principality of Monaco in southern France is the world's most densely populated country, with 42,840 people per square mile. **C6**

The smallest country in Western Europe—and the entire world—is Vatican City, which lies within the Italian capital of Rome. It produces its own coins and stamps and, because it is the home of the pope, it is the center of the entire Roman Catholic Church. **D7**

Switzerland has the highest rate of glass recycling in the world at 91 percent.

Fact file

Largest country France: 213,137 sq. mi.

Largest population Germany: 82,431,400

Biggest city London, England: 7,465,100 people **B5**

Highest point Mont Blanc, Alps, France: 15,771 ft. **B6**

Lowest point Zuidplaspolder, Netherlands, and Lammefjord, Denmark: 23 ft. below sea level **C6–C5**

Longest river Rhine: 825 mi.

27   28

Wild boar are found in Europe's forests and grasslands, living in groups of up to 50. These nocturnal creatures search for food but often destroy farmers' crops. They are good swimmers and fast runners and have sharp tusks, which can make them dangerous if cornered.

Lippizaners are the oldest breed of European horse. These graceful horses are named after the Slovenian farm where they were first bred. Today they are bred in the Spanish Riding School in Vienna, Austria, where they are trained to perform tricks.

Vineyards dot the hilly slopes of Europe from Austria to France, producing grapes from which wine is made and sold across the world. The quality of grapes grown and the taste of the wine is affected by the vineyard's soil and how much sun the vines receive during the year.

David, a statue of the biblical hero, stands over 14 feet tall. It was created by the Italian painter, sculptor, and architect Michelangelo (1475–1564), who lived and worked during a time of great cultural and intellectual activity known as the Renaissance.

The Guggenheim Museum in Bilbao, Spain, was designed by American architect Frank O. Gehry in 1997. It contains 19 galleries covering some 120,000 square feet—that's almost the size of two football fields. The museum attracts nearly 1 million people each year.

EASTERN EUROPE

EASTERN AND CENTRAL EUROPE has been a region of changing national boundaries over the years. The area contains some of the world's youngest nations, many of which were created after the collapse of the Soviet Union and the breakup of Yugoslavia in the early 1990s. There are also the remains of some of the world's oldest civilizations, such as ancient Greece. This culture flourished throughout the eastern Mediterranean nearly 3,000 years ago, from 900 to 323 BC. To the east, the enormous country of Russia spans the two continents of Europe and Asia. The Ural Mountains, which run through the middle of Russia, are considered by many to be the dividing line between these two continents. Also stretching to the east is a large area of grassland, called the steppes, which runs for nearly 5,000 miles in a huge belt from Hungary in the west, through the Ukraine and Russia, and to Mongolia and China in the east.

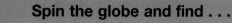
Spin the globe and find . . .
Locate Moscow at these coordinates: 55°N latitude, 37°E longitude.
- How many countries have a coastline on the Black Sea?
- What countries lie directly to the west of Poland?

The Cathedral of St. Basil is a large church at one end of Red Square, Moscow, Russia. It was completed in 1560 by the Russian ruler, or tsar, Ivan IV, who was known as "Ivan the Terrible." Before the fall of the Soviet Union, Red Square was the site of parades held each year to celebrate May Day and the October Revolution.

NORTHERN

SOUTHERN

The Acropolis in Athens, Greece, was used by the ancient Greeks as a fort and as a temple to the goddess Athena. *Acropolis* means "highest part of the town" in Greek and the building rises about 197 feet above the city. Ancient Greece introduced the concepts of democracy and philosophy, as well as the Olympic Games, which were first held in Greece in 776 BC.

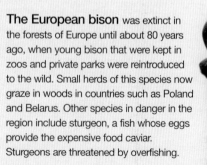

The European bison was extinct in the forests of Europe until about 80 years ago, when young bison that were kept in zoos and private parks were reintroduced to the wild. Small herds of this species now graze in woods in countries such as Poland and Belarus. Other species in danger in the region include sturgeon, a fish whose eggs provide the expensive food caviar. Sturgeons are threatened by overfishing.

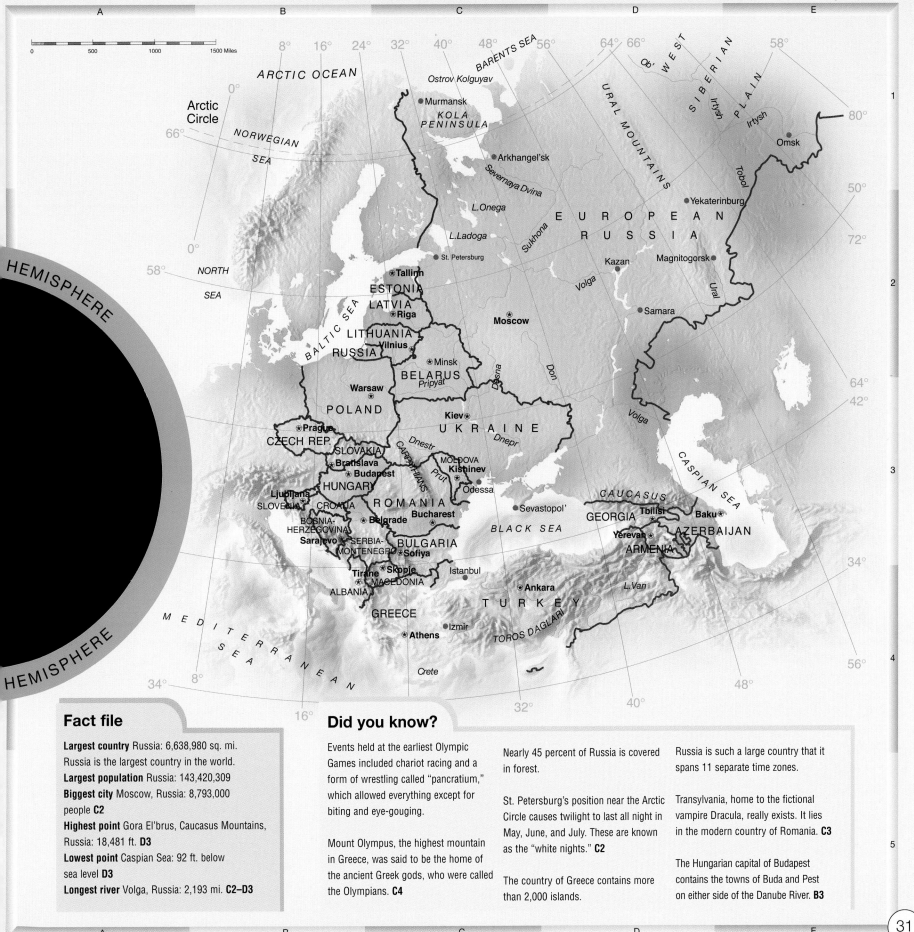

Fact file

Largest country Russia: 6,638,980 sq. mi. Russia is the largest country in the world.

Largest population Russia: 143,420,309

Biggest city Moscow, Russia: 8,793,000 people **C2**

Highest point Gora El'brus, Caucasus Mountains, Russia: 18,481 ft. **D3**

Lowest point Caspian Sea: 92 ft. below sea level **D3**

Longest river Volga, Russia: 2,193 mi. **C2–D3**

Did you know?

Events held at the earliest Olympic Games included chariot racing and a form of wrestling called "pancratium," which allowed everything except for biting and eye-gouging.

Mount Olympus, the highest mountain in Greece, was said to be the home of the ancient Greek gods, who were called the Olympians. **C4**

Nearly 45 percent of Russia is covered in forest.

St. Petersburg's position near the Arctic Circle causes twilight to last all night in May, June, and July. These are known as the "white nights." **C2**

The country of Greece contains more than 2,000 islands.

Russia is such a large country that it spans 11 separate time zones.

Transylvania, home to the fictional vampire Dracula, really exists. It lies in the modern country of Romania. **C3**

The Hungarian capital of Budapest contains the towns of Buda and Pest on either side of the Danube River. **B3**

Northern Africa

Lying just above the equator, the northern part of the African continent is dominated by the Sahara, the world's largest desert. It stretches for 3,000 miles from east to west and for 1,200 miles from north to south. Much of the desert is covered in stones and rocks; only 25 percent is covered in sand. A few underground rivers from the Atlas Mountains and water from the Nile and Niger rivers bring water to oases in the otherwise dry desert. People have been living alongside the Nile for thousands of years. The ancient Egyptians flourished here from about 3000 BC, building enormous cities, monuments, and temples, including the pyramids at Giza and the Temple of Luxor.

Spin the globe and find . . .

Locate Cairo at these coordinates: 30°N latitude, 31°E longitude.

- Which African countries lie on the Tropic of Cancer?
- Running between Port Said and Suez in Egypt, the Suez Canal links which seas?

NORTHERN

SOUTHERN

The Great Pyramid at Giza, Egypt, was built from roughly 2.5 million blocks of limestone for the pharaoh Kufu around 2580 BC. Egyptian pyramids were enormous tombs and were thought to provide a gateway for pharaohs to move to the next world. The body of the pharaoh would be preserved before burial by removing the internal organs and wrapping the body in linen bandages.

Camels have been used in hot and dusty regions such as Africa for centuries to carry people and heavy loads through scorching deserts. Camels are well suited to the searing heat and dust. They have fur-lined ears that filter out sand and long eyelashes to protect the camel's eyes from dust. They can also survive for up to a week without food or water.

The Nile is the world's longest river. It begins in Uganda, where the White Nile starts, and Ethiopia, where the Blue Nile starts. The two rivers meet in Khartoum, Sudan, and flow north to Egypt and the Mediterranean. The Nile regularly floods the surrounding landscape, depositing nutrients and making the soil ideal for growing crops. Traditional boats, called feluccas, are used to sail up and down the river.

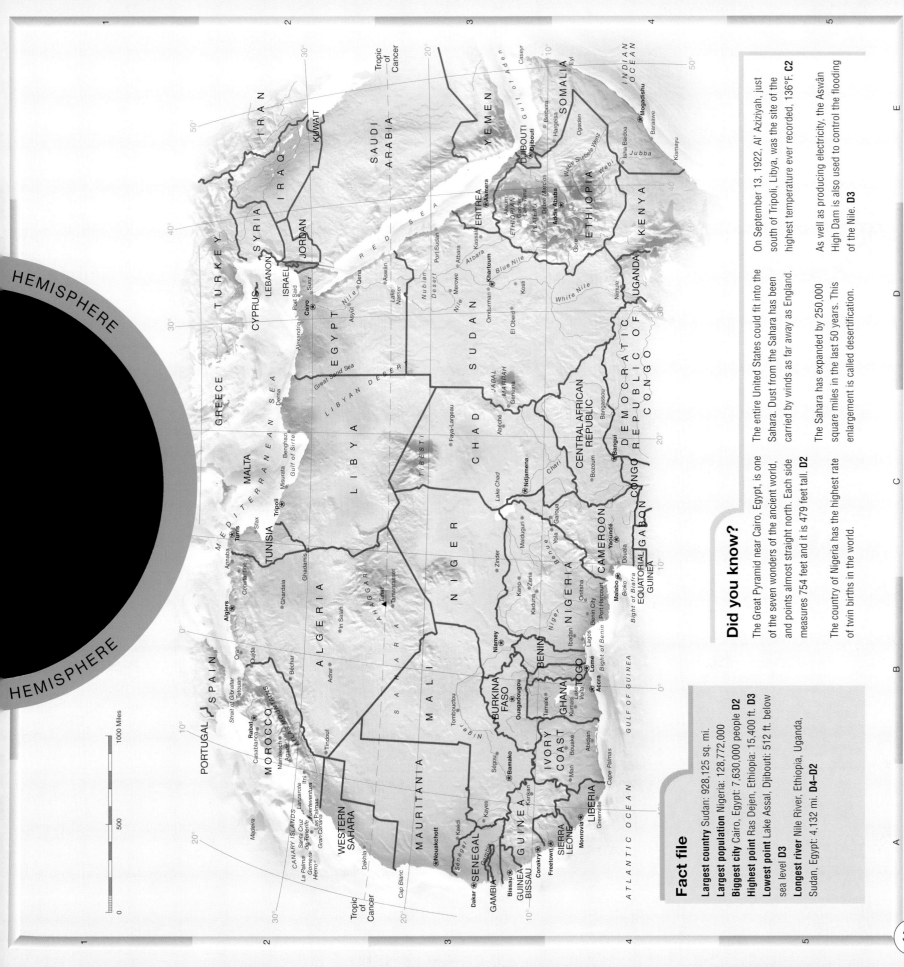

HEMISPHERE

HEMISPHERE

Fact file

Largest country Sudan: 928,125 sq. mi.

Largest population Nigeria: 128,772,000

Biggest city Cairo, Egypt: 7,630,000 people **D2**

Highest point Ras Dejen, Ethiopia: 15,400 ft. **D3**

Lowest point Lake Assal, Djibouti: 512 ft. below sea level **D3**

Longest river Nile River, Ethiopia, Uganda, Sudan, Egypt: 4,132 mi. **D4–D2**

Did you know?

The Great Pyramid near Cairo, Egypt, is one of the seven wonders of the ancient world, and points almost straight north. Each side measures 754 feet and it is 479 feet tall. **D2**

The country of Nigeria has the highest rate of twin births in the world.

The entire United States could fit into the Sahara. Dust from the Sahara has been carried by winds as far away as England. **D2**

The Sahara has expanded by 250,000 square miles in the last 50 years. This enlargement is called desertification.

On September 13, 1922, Al' Azīzīyah, just south of Tripoli, Libya, was the site of the highest temperature ever recorded, 136°F. **C2**

As well as producing electricity, the Aswān High Dam is also used to control the flooding of the Nile. **D3**

SOUTHERN AFRICA

MASSIVE, OPEN GRASSY PLAINS, called savannas, cover much of southern Africa. These vast plains are home to enormous herds of animals, including zebras, antelope, and wildebeests, which travel hundreds of miles in long journeys, called migrations, in a desperate search for food and water. For part of the year, little or no rain falls on the plains. During these dry seasons, food and water become scarce and the animals group together around the few remaining sources, forming enormous herds of thousands of creatures. Lying off the southeastern coast of Africa is the large island of Madagascar. This island has been separated from Africa for millions of years; this has allowed the evolution of many unique animals, including primates such as the aye-aye and 40 different species of lemurs.

Spin the globe and find . . .

Locate Kinshasa at these coordinates: 5°S latitude, 15°E longitude.

- How many African countries lie on the equator?
- What ocean surrounds the island of Madagascar?

Nelson Mandela spent his life fighting the racist politics of South Africa, which was governed by the system of apartheid. Black people were oppressed and treated poorly by the white minority. Mandela was imprisoned from 1962 to 1990. Following his release and the removal of the apartheid system, he was elected prime minister in 1994, a position he held until 1999.

NORTHERN

SOUTHERN

Kilimanjaro is the highest mountain in Africa and lies in northeastern Tanzania. The mountain itself was formed by three volcanoes (now extinct) that rose out of the surrounding plain. The summit is covered in snow and ice all year round. However, global warming has led to the melting of much of Kilimanjaro's glacier, and some scientists fear the glacier will disappear altogether in 15 years.

Diamond mining is a major industry in southern Africa. Diamonds were first discovered in South Africa near the town of Kimberley around 1870 and this sparked off a rush of people moving to the area in the hope of becoming rich. The Kimberley Mine was once the richest diamond-producing mine in the world. Although closed today, the huge hole remains and measures over 700 feet deep and 0.9 miles around.

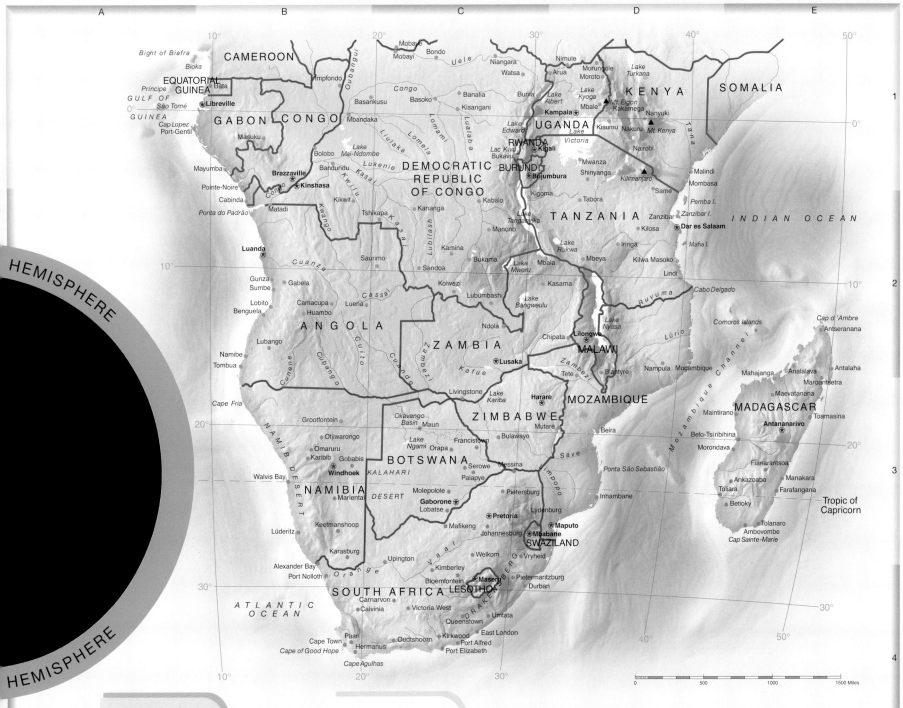

HEMISPHERE

HEMISPHERE

Bight of Biafra
CAMEROON
Bioka
EQUATORIAL
GUINEA
Príncipe Bata
GULF OF São Tomé ★ Libreville
GUINEA Cap Lopez
Port-Gentil

GABON CONGO

Mayumba
Masuku

Pointe-Noire ★ Brazzaville
Cabinda ★ Kinshasa
Matadi

Luanda

Gunza
Sumbe Gabela
Lobito
Benguela Camacupa
Huambo

ANGOLA

Lubango

Namibe
Tombua

Cape Fria

Grootfontein

Otjiwarongo
Omaruru
Karibib Gobabis
Walvis Bay ★ Windhoek KALAHARI
Swakopmund

NAMIBIA DESERT
Mariental

Keetmanshoop

Lüderitz

Karasburg

Alexander Bay Upington
Port Nolloth Orange

ATLANTIC Carnarvon
OCEAN Calvinia Victoria West

Cape Town Paarl
Cape of Good Hope Hermanus Oudtshoorn
Cape Agulhas

Mobaye
Mobayi Bondo
Uele
Niangara Nimule Morungole
Watsa Arua Moroto Lake Turkana
Impfondo Banalia Bunia Lake Morungole
Basankusu Basoko Kisangani Lake Albert Kampala Mbale Mt. Elgon KENYA SOMALIA
Mbandaka Lake Kyoga Kakamega Nanyuki
Congo Lake Edward UGANDA Kisumu Nakuru Mt. Kenya
Lake RWANDA Lake Nairobi Tana
Mai-Ndombe Bolobo Bukavu Lac Kivu ★ Kigali Victoria
Bandundu BURUNDI Mwanza Malindi
Kikwit DEMOCRATIC ★ Bujumbura Shinyanga Kilimanjaro Mombasa
REPUBLIC Kigoma Pemba I.
Kananga OF CONGO Tabora TANZANIA Zanzibar I.
Tshikapa Kabalo Lake Zanzibar Same
Saurimo Kamina Tanganyika Kilosa ★ Dar es Salaam INDIAN OCEAN
Manono Mafia I.
Sandoa Lake Iringa
Kolwezi Mweru Mbeya Kilwa Masoko
Lubumbashi Lake Lindi
Ndola Bangweulu Kasama Ruvuma Cabo Delgado
ZAMBIA Lake Chipata Lake Comoros Islands Cap d'Ambre
★ Lusaka Mbala Nyasa Antseranana
Kafue ★ Lilongwe Lúrio
Livingstone Lake Kariba Tete MALAWI Nampula Moçambique Mahajanga Analalava Antalaha
Okavango Maun Harare Blantyre MOZAMBIQUE Maroantsetra
Basin ZIMBABWE Mutare Maevatanana
Lake Francistown Bulawayo Beira MADAGASCAR
Ngami Orapa Save Maintirano Belo-Tsiribihina Antananarivo ★
BOTSWANA Serowe Messina Ponta São Sebastião Morondava Fianarantsoa Tropic of
★ Gaborone Palapye Capricorn
Molepolole Pietersburg Inhambane Ankazoabo Manakara
Lobatse ★ Pretoria Lydenburg Toliara Farafangana
Mafikeng ★ Maputo Betioky
Johannesburg Mbabane Tolanaro
SWAZILAND Ambovombe
Welkom Vryheid Cap Sainte-Marie
Kimberley ★ Maseru Pietermaritzburg
Bloemfontein LESOTHO Durban
SOUTH AFRICA
Umtata
Queenstown
Kirkwood East London
Port Alfred
Port Elizabeth

0 500 1000 1500 Miles

35

Fact file

Largest country Democratic Republic of Congo: 885,780 sq. mi.

Largest population Democratic Republic of Congo: 60,085,800

Biggest city Kinshasa, Democratic Republic of Congo: 6,789,900 people **B1**

Highest point Mount Kilimanjaro, Tanzania: 19,340 ft. **D1**

Lowest point Atlantic and Indian oceans: 0 ft.

Longest river Congo River: 2,900 mi. **C1–B2**

Did you know?

Nearly 40 percent of the continent of Africa is covered in savanna.

The African elephant is the largest living land animal, weighing up to 9 tons.

The aye-aye, which lives on Madagascar, eats grubs that it picks out of tree bark with an extremely long, thin finger on each hand.

Lake Victoria is the largest lake in Africa. It covers an area of 26,828 square miles and lies within Tanzania and Uganda. **D1**

Victoria Falls lies on the Zambezi River, **C3**. The waterfall is twice as big as Niagara Falls. Local people call the falls *Mosi-oa-Tunya*, which means "the smoke that thunders."

The movement of the massive plates that make up the Earth's crust is pulling the western side of the region away from the eastern side at a rate of $^{1}/_{4}$ inch every year. This movement has caused an enormous series of cracks that run for 6,000 miles, known as the Great Rift Valley. The south part in eastern Africa contains the deepest lakes and highest mountains in Uganda, Kenya, and Malawi.

THE MIDDLE EAST

THE MIDDLE EAST, WHICH LIES BETWEEN AFRICA AND EUROPE, has been an important region for three of the world's main religions: Islam, Judaism, and Christianity. The area has many cities and sites that one or more of these religions considers sacred, and that are thousands of years old, such as Jerusalem and Mecca. Huge reserves of oil lie buried beneath the ground and the profits that come from drilling for oil and turning it into gasoline has made some countries in the region very wealthy. The area has a very dry climate and freshwater is a scarce resource—only Iran and Turkey have significant freshwater sources. As a result, many countries use seawater as a resource. The salt has to be taken out using special factories, called desalination plants, where the seawater is heated to separate the salt from the water.

Spin the globe and find . . .

Locate the country of Kuwait at these coordinates: 29°N latitude, 45°E longitude.

- What inland sea lies to the north of Iran?
- What city lies at the point where the Mediterranean Sea and the Black Sea meet?

The Dead Sea is so salty that people can easily float in it. The extra salt makes the water denser than normal water, so it can support objects more easily. People are attracted to health spas around the Dead Sea because the salts are said to have health-giving properties.

NORTHERN

SOUTHERN

Jerusalem in Israel is a sacred place for Jews, Christians, and Muslims and contains many sites that are considered holy by each religion. These include the Dome of the Rock, which is an important Jewish and Muslim site and can be seen in the background in this picture. The Wailing Wall lies in the foreground of this picture and is an important Jewish site, while the Church of the Holy Sepulchre (not seen here) is an important Christian site.

The Rub' al-Khali, or Empty Quarter, in the Arabian Peninsula is the world's largest sand desert and features sand dunes over 1,000 feet high, which is higher than the Eiffel Tower. Fierce winds blow through the area and create these huge, shifting sand dunes. The temperatures drop below freezing at night and soar to over 130°F at noon, and many months can pass without a single drop of rain falling.

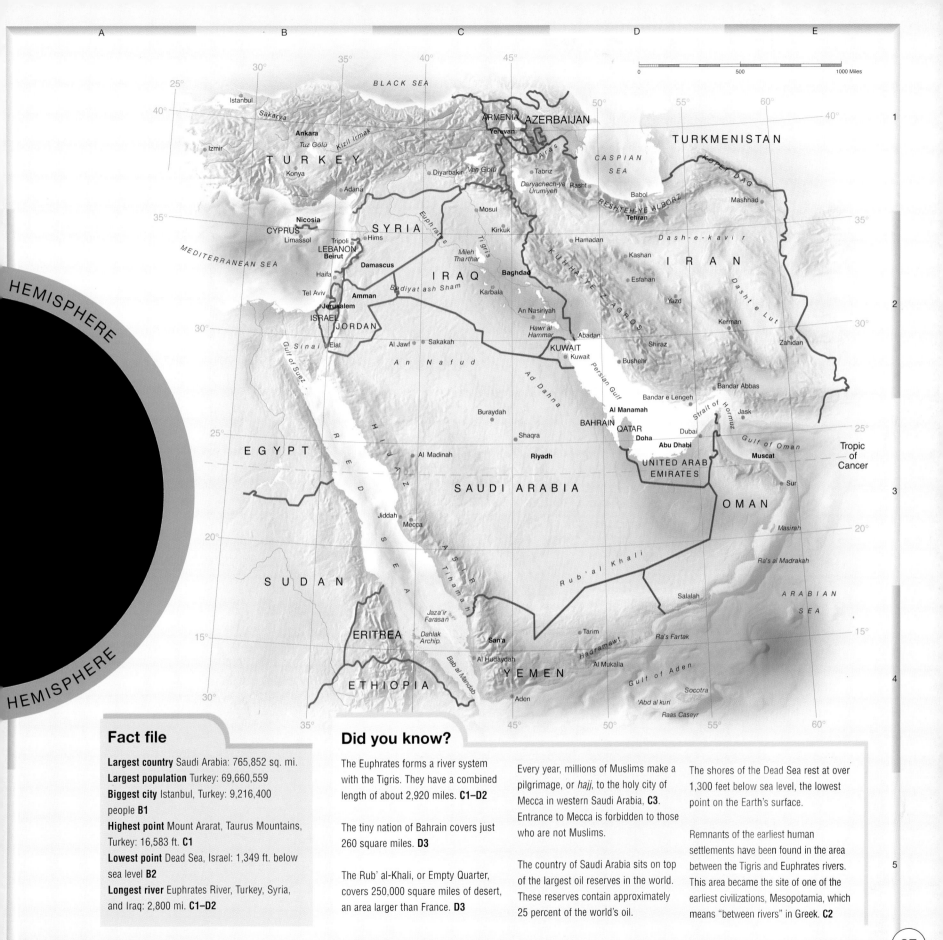

Fact file

Largest country Saudi Arabia: 765,852 sq. mi.

Largest population Turkey: 69,660,559

Biggest city Istanbul, Turkey: 9,216,400 people **B1**

Highest point Mount Ararat, Taurus Mountains, Turkey: 16,583 ft. **C1**

Lowest point Dead Sea, Israel: 1,349 ft. below sea level **B2**

Longest river Euphrates River, Turkey, Syria, and Iraq: 2,800 mi. **C1–D2**

Did you know?

The Euphrates forms a river system with the Tigris. They have a combined length of about 2,920 miles. **C1–D2**

The tiny nation of Bahrain covers just 260 square miles. **D3**

The Rub' al-Khali, or Empty Quarter, covers 250,000 square miles of desert, an area larger than France. **D3**

Every year, millions of Muslims make a pilgrimage, or *hajj*, to the holy city of Mecca in western Saudi Arabia, **C3**. Entrance to Mecca is forbidden to those who are not Muslims.

The country of Saudi Arabia sits on top of the largest oil reserves in the world. These reserves contain approximately 25 percent of the world's oil.

The shores of the Dead Sea rest at over 1,300 feet below sea level, the lowest point on the Earth's surface.

Remnants of the earliest human settlements have been found in the area between the Tigris and Euphrates rivers. This area became the site of one of the earliest civilizations, Mesopotamia, which means "between rivers" in Greek. **C2**

CENTRAL ASIA

THIS REGION contains a mixture of ancient civilizations and modern societies. The cultures of China and Japan date back thousands of years, and the region is dotted with palaces and monuments such as the Great Wall of China and the Himeji Castle in Japan. Today, Japan leads the world in many high-tech industries, including computers and robotics. The eastern edge of the region experiences many natural disasters, including earthquakes, volcanic eruptions, and raging typhoons. To the west, the land contains the cold Gobi Desert and vast steppes that stretch all the way to Europe. To the south lie the Himalayas, the "roof of the world." This mountain range contains the highest peaks on Earth, including Mount Everest, which is over 29,000 feet high.

Spin the globe and find . . .

Locate Tokyo at these coordinates: 35°N latitude, 140°E longitude.

- Into which sea does the Chang Jiang River empty?
- How many countries share a border with China?

NORTHERN

SOUTHERN

Pandas are related to bears and live high up in the mountain forests of central China. They are restricted in their habitat, as their diet is mainly bamboo shoots and leaves. They use their paws and a thumblike bone to grip the bamboo stems. Cutting down forests for logging or farming destroys the bamboo supplies and threatens this endangered creature.

The Great Wall of China was built over 2,000 years ago to defend China from attack. It winds its way from east to west through China's mountains, valleys, and grasslands. The wall is 4,500 miles long and was constructed by an army of soldiers, prisoners, and local people at a rate of 1/2 mile per day!

Hong Kong is a large, bustling city on the southern coast of China. Formerly a colony of Great Britain, the city has grown rapidly over the last 200 years as a center for trade and commerce between Southeast Asia and the rest of the world. On midnight of July 1, 1997, Hong Kong was handed back to Chinese rule.

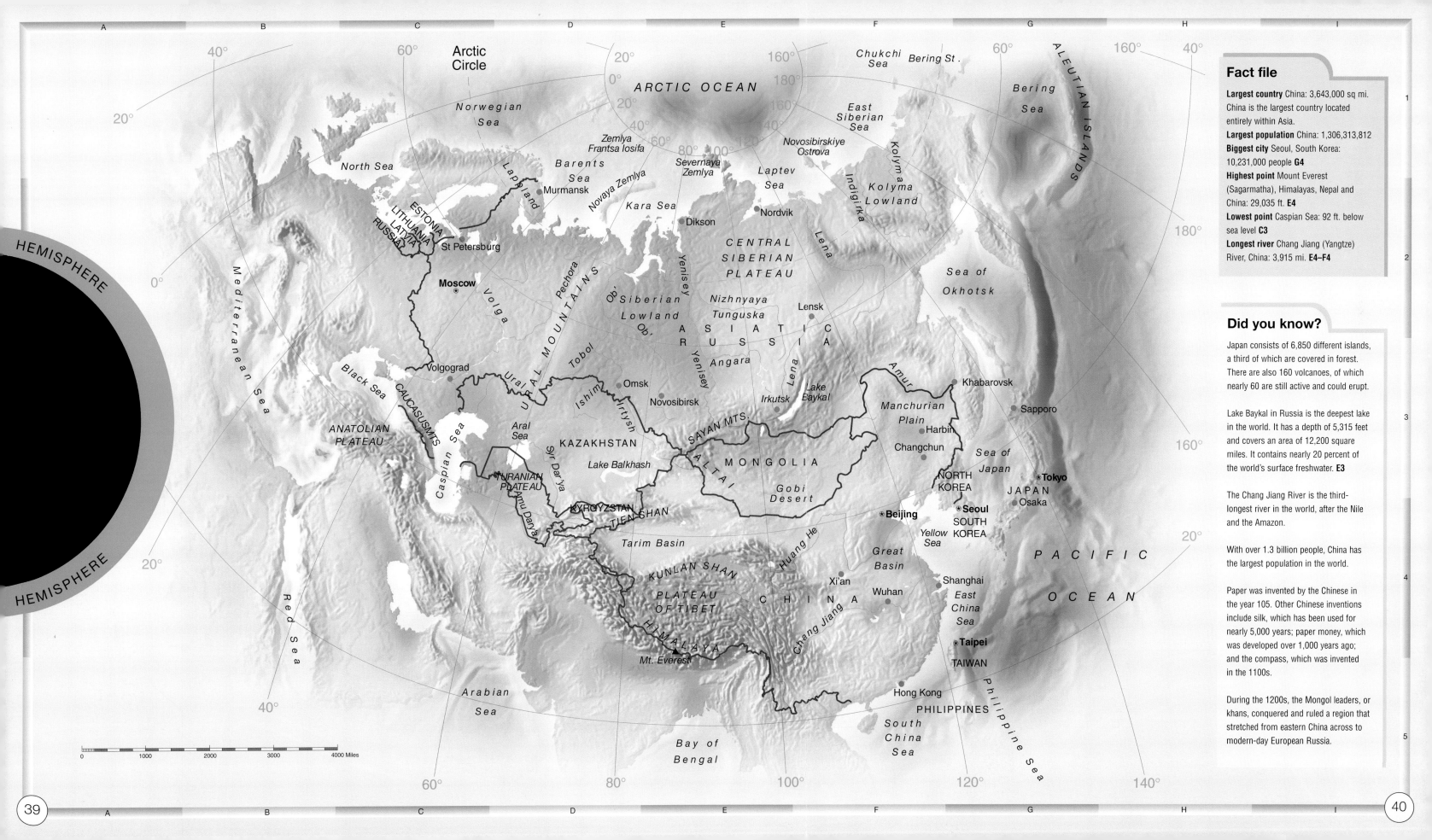

Arctic Circle

ARCTIC OCEAN

Chukchi Sea   Bering St.

Bering Sea

ALEUTIAN ISLANDS

Norwegian Sea

Zemlya Frantsa Iosifa

Barents Sea

Novaya Zemlya

Severnaya Zemlya

East Siberian Sea

Kara Sea

Novosibirskiye Ostrova

Laptev Sea

Kolyma Lowland

North Sea

Murmansk

Indigirka

Kolyma

ESTONIA
LITHUANIA
LATVIA
RUSSIA

St Petersburg

Dikson

Nordvik

CENTRAL SIBERIAN PLATEAU

Lena

Sea of Okhotsk

Mediterranean Sea

Moscow

Volga

Pechora

U R A L   M O U N T A I N S

Ob'

Siberian Lowland

Nizhnyaya Tunguska

Ob'

A S I A T I C

Lensk

R U S S I A

Volgograd

Ural

Tobol

Yenisey

Ishim

Irtysh

Yenisey

Angara

Lena

Khabarovsk

Black Sea

CAUCASUS MTS.

Caspian Sea

Aral Sea

Omsk

Novosibirsk

Irkutsk

Lake Baykal

Amur

Manchurian Plain

Sapporo

ANATOLIAN PLATEAU

KAZAKHSTAN

SAYAN MTS.

MONGOLIA

Harbin

Changchun

Sea of Japan

Tokyo

Syr Dar'ya

Lake Balkhash

A L T A I

Gobi Desert

NORTH KOREA

JAPAN

Osaka

TURANIAN PLATEAU

Amu Darya

KYRGYZSTAN

TIEN SHAN

Beijing

Seoul

SOUTH KOREA

Yellow Sea

Tarim Basin

Huang He

Great Basin

Red Sea

KUNLAN SHAN

PLATEAU OF TIBET

C H I N A

Xi'an

Wuhan

Shanghai

East China Sea

PACIFIC OCEAN

HIMALAYA

Mt. Everest

Chang Jiang

Taipei

TAIWAN

Arabian Sea

Hong Kong

PHILIPPINES

Philippine Sea

Bay of Bengal

South China Sea

Fact file

Largest country China: 3,643,000 sq mi. China is the largest country located entirely within Asia.

Largest population China: 1,306,313,812

Biggest city Seoul, South Korea: 10,231,000 people **G4**

Highest point Mount Everest (Sagarmatha), Himalayas, Nepal and China: 29,035 ft. **E4**

Lowest point Caspian Sea: 92 ft. below sea level **C3**

Longest river Chang Jiang (Yangtze) River, China: 3,915 mi. **E4–F4**

Did you know?

Japan consists of 6,850 different islands, a third of which are covered in forest. There are also 160 volcanoes, of which nearly 60 are still active and could erupt.

Lake Baykal in Russia is the deepest lake in the world. It has a depth of 5,315 feet and covers an area of 12,200 square miles. It contains nearly 20 percent of the world's surface freshwater. **E3**

The Chang Jiang River is the third-longest river in the world, after the Nile and the Amazon.

With over 1.3 billion people, China has the largest population in the world.

Paper was invented by the Chinese in the year 105. Other Chinese inventions include silk, which has been used for nearly 5,000 years; paper money, which was developed over 1,000 years ago; and the compass, which was invented in the 1100s.

During the 1200s, the Mongol leaders, or khans, conquered and ruled a region that stretched from eastern China across to modern-day European Russia.

0   1000   2000   3000   4000 Miles

A robot toy from Japan. Japan leads the way in many technological industries, including computers, television, and robotics. Not only are robots made as toys to entertain children, but they are also used in factories to make everything from washing machines to cars and even other robots!

This high-speed bullet train is at the forefront of Japanese technology. It speeds along at an average of 164 mph, linking Japan's main island of Honshu with the capital of Tokyo. Japanese engineers are currently developing a train that travels even faster than the bullet train and floats above the tracks using magnets. It is called a maglev train.

Mount Everest, or Sagarmatha, is the world's highest peak and is part of the Himalayas. The range was created when two of the earth's plates crashed into each other. As the plates continue to move, the Himalayas grow by about an inch each year! Many people attempt to scale the peak, but the climb is dangerous. In 1996, 19 people died while trying to reach the summit.

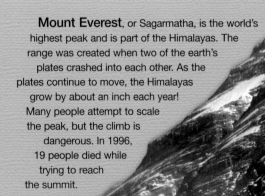

The Siberian tiger is usually found in cold, snow-covered areas such as the icy taiga of Siberia, which is covered in evergreen forests. It is the largest of the big cats and has a longer fur coat than other tigers. To survive the cold, the Siberian tiger eats about 20 pounds of food a day, including prey such as deer and wild boar.

SOUTHERN ASIA

SOUTHERN ASIA COVERS THE INDIAN SUBCONTINENT, which includes the countries of India, Pakistan, Nepal, Bhutan, and Bangladesh. It is separated from the rest of Asia by the massive, towering mountain ranges of the Himalayas and Hindu Kush. To the southeast are thousands of islands, many of which are fringed by sandy beaches. Tourists are attracted to southern Asia by these beaches as well as the hot weather, warm seas, abundant wildlife, and rain forests. They also come to see many ancient buildings and monuments, such as the Taj Mahal in India. A seasonal wind, or monsoon, blows across India and Bangladesh, bringing weeks of torrential rains followed by dry seasons. The whole region is vulnerable to severe environmental conditions as well as to cyclones and tsunamis.

Spin the globe and find . . .

Locate Singapore at these coordinates: 1°N latitude, 103°E longitude.

● What countries lie around the Bay of Bengal?

● Trace the path of the Mekong River and find the country in which it originates.

Asian elephants are smaller than African elephants, with smaller ears and a fourth toenail on each hind foot. Asian elephants live in the wild and are also used as working animals. They can carry heavy loads on their backs and lift large objects weighing up to 550 pounds using their trunks.

NORTHERN

SOUTHERN

The Taj Mahal is one of the most recognized structures in India and is one of its key tourist attractions. It was built in Agra in the 1600s by the Mughal emperor Shah Jahan as a memorial to his wife, who died in childbirth. Agra was the capital of the Mughals, a Muslim empire that ruled northern India between the 1500s and 1800s.

Rice plants are often grown in flooded fields, called paddies, or in fields cut into mountainsides to form terraces. They are also grown alongside rivers. Rice was first cultivated around 3500 BC. It is the staple food for over 65 percent of India's population and growing rice is a major source of employment throughout southern Asia.

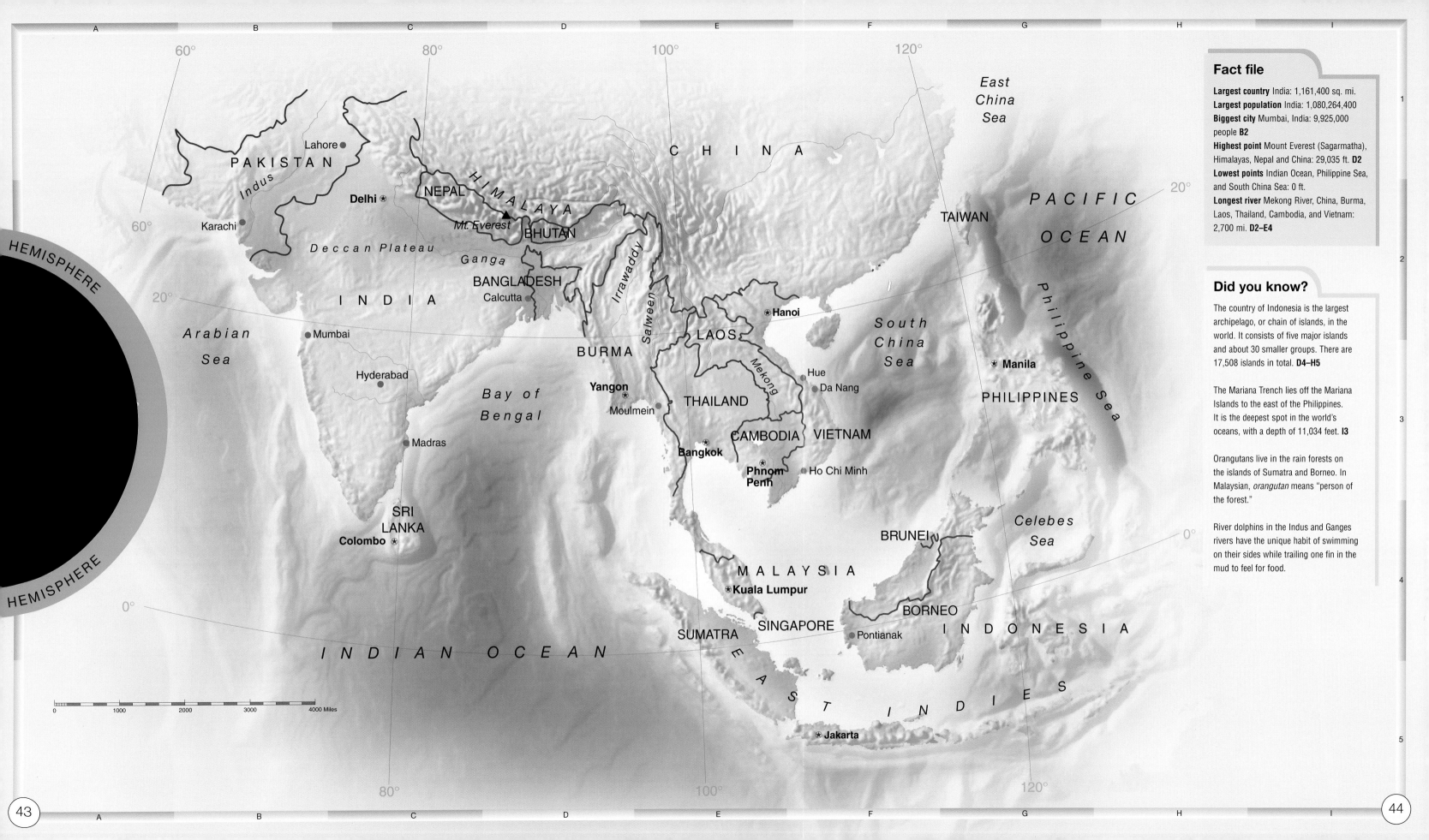

A | **B** | **C** | **D** | **E** | **F** | **G** | **H** | **I**

60°   80°   100°   120°

East China Sea

PAKISTAN

Lahore

Indus

Delhi ✳

Karachi

NEPAL   *HIMALAYA*

Mt. Everest

BHUTAN

C H I N A

20°

PACIFIC OCEAN

Deccan Plateau

Ganga

BANGLADESH

Calcutta

I N D I A

Irrawaddy

Salween

TAIWAN

20°

LAOS

Hanoi ✳

South China Sea

Arabian Sea

Mumbai

Hyderabad

Bay of Bengal

BURMA

Yangon

Moulmein

Mekong

THAILAND

Hue

Da Nang

Philippine Sea

✳ **Manila**

Madras

CAMBODIA

VIETNAM

PHILIPPINES

Bangkok ✳

Phnom Penh

Ho Chi Minh

SRI LANKA

Celebes Sea

Colombo ✳

BRUNEI

0°

MALAYSIA

✳ **Kuala Lumpur**

BORNEO

INDONESIA

SINGAPORE

Pontianak

SUMATRA

I N D I A N   O C E A N

E A S T   I N D I E S

✳ **Jakarta**

0   1000   2000   3000   4000 Miles

HEMISPHERE

HEMISPHERE

60°

20°

0°

80°

100°

120°

Fact file

Largest country India: 1,161,400 sq. mi.
Largest population India: 1,080,264,400
Biggest city Mumbai, India: 9,925,000 people **B2**
Highest point Mount Everest (Sagarmatha), Himalayas, Nepal and China: 29,035 ft. **D2**
Lowest points Indian Ocean, Philippine Sea, and South China Sea: 0 ft.
Longest river Mekong River, China, Burma, Laos, Thailand, Cambodia, and Vietnam: 2,700 mi. **D2–E4**

Did you know?

The country of Indonesia is the largest archipelago, or chain of islands, in the world. It consists of five major islands and about 30 smaller groups. There are 17,508 islands in total. **D4–H5**

The Mariana Trench lies off the Mariana Islands to the east of the Philippines. It is the deepest spot in the world's oceans, with a depth of 11,034 feet. **I3**

Orangutans live in the rain forests on the islands of Sumatra and Borneo. In Malaysian, *orangutan* means "person of the forest."

River dolphins in the Indus and Ganges rivers have the unique habit of swimming on their sides while trailing one fin in the mud to feel for food.

Cricket is one of the most popular sports in India, Pakistan, Bangladesh, and Sri Lanka. The game involves two teams of 11 players with one side batting and the other fielding. Children play games in the streets or on beaches, while professionals compete in matches around the world. Other popular sports played in the region include polo, which was started in Pakistan, and field hockey.

The floating market in Bangkok, Thailand, is a market on water. By eight o'clock in the morning, market sellers paddle up and down the city's canals to get the best positions. The canals were built in the 19th century to help ease travel across the city. Today the floating market is a tourist attraction, but many people also live and work along the bustling canals.

Singapore is the busiest port in southern Asia and is a major economic force in the region. The island combines ancient Asian traditions, such as junk boats, with modern skyscrapers and shopping malls. Singapore is home to a diverse mix of people who celebrate their various religions, including Taoism, Buddhism, Islam, Christianity, and Hinduism, with festivals enjoyed by all.

The Komodo dragon is found on a few Indonesian islands and is the world's largest lizard. It grows up to 10 feet long and sprints for short bursts, bringing down its prey, such as a deer, wild boar, or monkeys, with a bite. The prey slowly dies from an infection that results from a bacteria that is found in the Komodo dragon's mouth.

Stilt houses are found lining the banks of the Mekong River, the longest river in southern Asia. The river provides food, transportation, communication, and housing to people in Vietnam. The stilt houses are built in the river on strong poles to keep them above the water level, and people use small boats to get to land.

OCEANIA

OCEANIA (OR AUSTRALASIA) INCLUDES Australia, New Zealand, New Guinea, and the islands in the Pacific. Australia is a large country of almost 3 million square miles. However, it is home to just 20 million people, many of whom live in a handful of cities around the coast. This leaves huge stretches of empty areas in the country's interior, a region known as the outback. Much of the outback is filled with tropical grassland areas and desert, which contrasts with the lush rain forests of the coastal regions and the north of the country. New Zealand consists of two large islands that contain volcanic landscapes with boiling mud and geysers as well as rich temperate rain forests, which are cooler than the tropical rain forests found in South America. The Pacific Ocean is dotted with thousands of small island nations such as Fiji.

Spin the globe and find . . .

Locate Sydney at these coordinates: 35°S latitude, 150°E longitude.

● What ocean lies off the west coast of Australia?

● What is the southernmost capital city in the world?

The Sydney Opera House sits on the harbor of Australia's capital city. Its sail-like roof was designed by Danish architect Jorn Utzon and was built in 1973. The opera house sits next to the Sydney Harbor Bridge and these two structures have become recognizable symbols of Australia and the focus of many international events and celebrations.

NORTHERN

SOUTHERN

Milford Sound, New Zealand, is a steep-sided flooded valley, or fjord. It is surrounded by mountains that rise 3,937 feet above the water and it was carved out by glaciers millions of years ago. It is located on New Zealand's South Island and forms part of Fiordland National Park. The park is a World Heritage Site, which gives it special protected status, and it has tumbling waterfalls and temperate rain forests.

The Great Barrier Reef is an enormous coral reef that stretches for more than 1,250 miles off the northeast coast of Australia. The reef is made from the skeletons of tiny creatures called coral polyps. This rich environment is home to a wide range of plants and animals, including fish, dolphins, sea snakes, and turtles.

Kangaroos are found in Australia and Papua New Guinea. They have strong hind legs and some can hop at speeds of up to 40 mph. They graze on grass and plants and can survive for months without water. Other animals that are found only in this region include koalas. Koalas are well adapted to the hot Australian climate and take in most of the water they need to live by eating the leaves of eucalyptus trees.

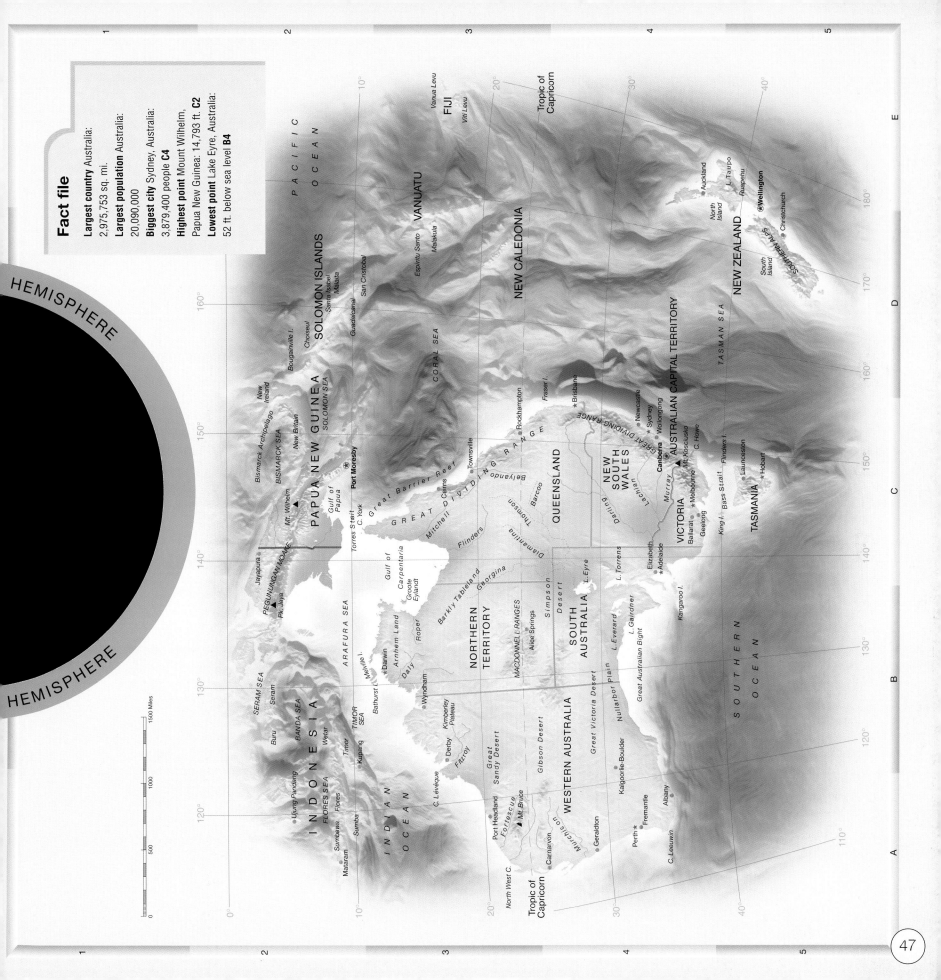

Fact file

Largest country Australia: 2,975,753 sq. mi.

Largest population Australia: 20,090,000

Biggest city Sydney, Australia: 3,879,400 people **C4**

Highest point Mount Wilhelm, Papua New Guinea: 14,793 ft. **C2**

Lowest point Lake Eyre, Australia: 52 ft. below sea level **B4**

THE ARCTIC AND ANTARCTICA

AT THE TOP AND BOTTOM OF OUR PLANET are cold, inhospitable regions: the Arctic and Antarctica. These places are covered in thick ice sheets all year round and see the sun for only half of the year. For six months, the sun does not rise above the horizon and the regions lie in freezing darkness. The area around the North Pole, called the Arctic, is a huge frozen sea with no mainland. It is surrounded by islands, such as Greenland, and the northern coasts of Canada, Asia, and Europe. Antarctica is the continent around the South Pole. This huge area of land is almost uninhabited except for people working in a number of scientific research stations. Despite the harsh conditions, there is a wide range of wildlife in the Arctic and Antarctica, including whales, fur seals, penguins, and tiny sea creatures called krill. Even small plants, such as lichen and moss, survive on the pieces of land that are free from ice.

Spin the globe and find . . .

Locate the Weddell Sea at these coordinates: 70°S latitude, 45°W longitude.

- What other continent is closest to Antarctica?
- What island is closest to the North Pole?

Penguins are flightless birds that live in the waters of the Southern Hemisphere. Many of them are found around Antarctica and they have a body shape that is perfectly adapted to life swimming in the icy water. They have thick layers of fat to protect them from the cold, as well as a coat of waterproof feathers.

NORTHERN

SOUTHERN

Icebergs are pieces of ice that break off from the thick ice sheets of the Arctic and Antarctica. They range in size from a few yards across to enormous blocks of ice—the largest ever found was as big as the state of Rhode Island. The icebergs drift away from the ice sheets and can be a hazard to ships. Scientists study icebergs to see how quickly the ice sheets are melting.

Polar bears live on ice sheets in the Arctic. They are the world's largest land carnivores and hunt seals, walruses, and reindeer. They are strong swimmers and have thick, waterproof, cream-colored fur and many layers of fat to keep them warm. Polar bears spend about half their time hunting but need to eat only about once every four or five days.

The Amundsen-Scott Base is located at the South Pole. The scientists based here study the atmosphere, the weather, and the ice sheets. During the summer months, they are supplied with food, water, and other goods by regular military flights. However, during the winter, when the sun never rises, no flights can land. A total of 27 different countries have research bases in Antarctica.

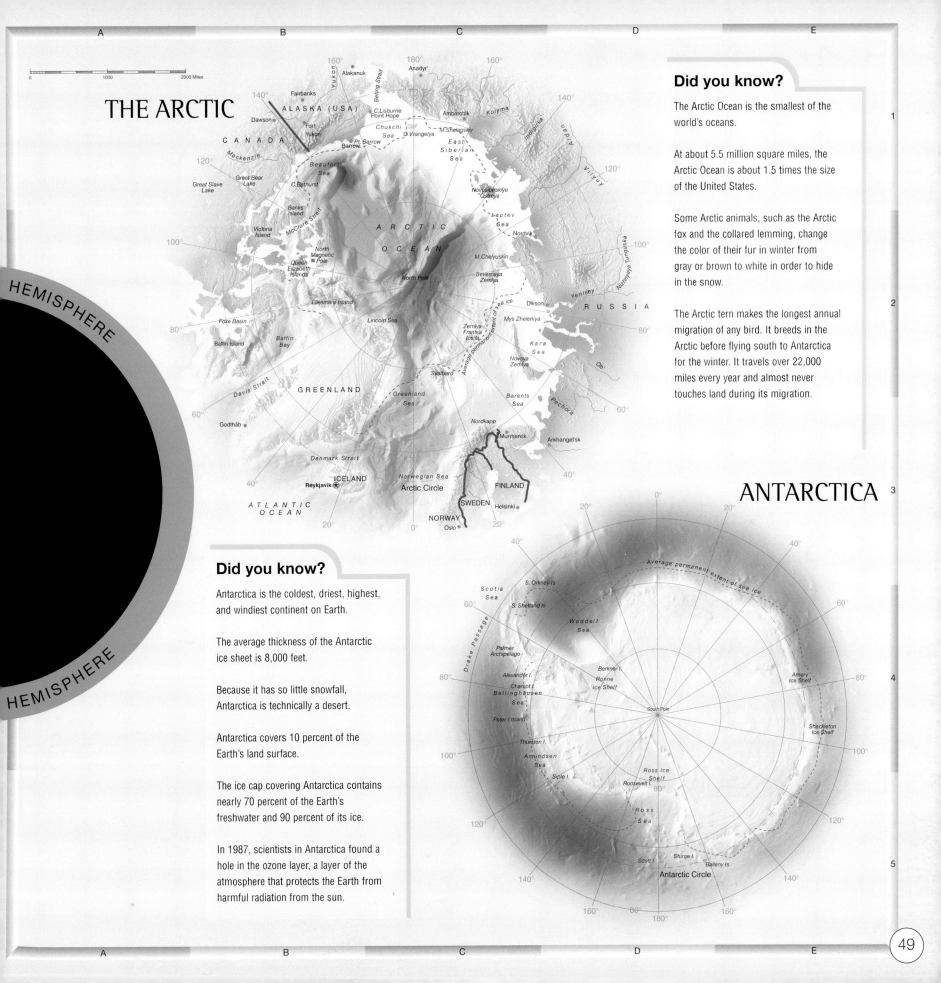

THE ARCTIC

ANTARCTICA

HEMISPHERE

HEMISPHERE

Did you know?

The Arctic Ocean is the smallest of the world's oceans.

At about 5.5 million square miles, the Arctic Ocean is about 1.5 times the size of the United States.

Some Arctic animals, such as the Arctic fox and the collared lemming, change the color of their fur in winter from gray or brown to white in order to hide in the snow.

The Arctic tern makes the longest annual migration of any bird. It breeds in the Arctic before flying south to Antarctica for the winter. It travels over 22,000 miles every year and almost never touches land during its migration.

Did you know?

Antarctica is the coldest, driest, highest, and windiest continent on Earth.

The average thickness of the Antarctic ice sheet is 8,000 feet.

Because it has so little snowfall, Antarctica is technically a desert.

Antarctica covers 10 percent of the Earth's land surface.

The ice cap covering Antarctica contains nearly 70 percent of the Earth's freshwater and 90 percent of its ice.

In 1987, scientists in Antarctica found a hole in the ozone layer, a layer of the atmosphere that protects the Earth from harmful radiation from the sun.

MAP REFERENCES

NORTHERN

SOUTHERN

50

HEMISPHERE

HEMISPHERE

INDEX

54